LANDING ON MY FEET
Learning to Lead Through Mentoring

ALISON MARTIN-BOOKS

President and CEO of Mentoring Women's Network

ISBN-13: 978-1492329572

ISBN-10: 1492329576

DEDICATION

This book is dedicated to the women who dare to dream and inspire others to do the same.

This book is also dedicated to my daughter Paiton. May she be courageous enough to pursue the life of her dreams and be her authentic, wonderful self.

ACKNOWLEDGEMENTS

I wish to acknowledge the many tremendous mentors and influencers I have had in my life.

In particular, the women whom I have met through my work with Mentoring Women's Network.

You have each enriched my life beyond measure and inspired me to write this book to encourage others to seek relationships with others who can serve as inspiration to uncover our true leadership potential.

TABLE OF CONTENTS

INTRODUCTION

I remember the first time I realized the impact mentoring had on my life and career. I was 29 years old and it was my first day on the job as executive director at a large nonprofit organization. The day began with a 7:30 a.m. meeting with some very influential CEOs, all of whom were male and at least twenty years my senior. I was on the agenda to speak with authority and passion about the project we were working on and the long-lasting impact it would have.

I was unbelievably nervous. As we walked from the parking garage to the board room, I caught a side glance of a reflection of myself and remember thinking, "How did I get here?" At that point, I looked over at my boss, who was also my mentor, and she gave me a reassuring smile.

Fortunately, I somehow managed to deliver the speech flawlessly and help reinvigorate the group toward a shared goal. We broke the record in our fundraising campaign that year, and I remain connected to many of the gentleman seated around the table that day.

Although I was only 29 years old, my journey moving up the ranks to the board room and beyond was a long one. I had faced plenty of obstacles and failures along the way. I was emancipated at the age of 17, and I dropped out of high school. I became a single mom at 18.

My success today can be attributed to a whole lot of hard work and the incredible willingness of others to offer me guidance along the way. Mentoring takes many forms; however, my goal is for everyone – men and women – to have the opportunity to know and experience what it means to learn from the knowledge and experience of others and to willingly share their knowledge and experience with others.

By learning and teaching to lead through mentoring, we can begin to address the gender gap by advancing more women leaders and helping to ensure that the next generation is prepared.

By owning our strengths and recognizing the strengths of others, we open ourselves to call upon the expertise of others for their support in our development, enabling us to lead more effectively. Those of us who regularly engage in mentoring can attest to the wonderful things that can result. As mentors, we find ourselves strengthening our communication and problem-solving skills while building incredible networks both inside and outside our companies.

My hope is this book will serve as inspiration to anyone daring enough to dream of a better life, willing to pursue her passions, and ready to let go of whatever is holding her back. By intentionally cultivating relationships with key individuals whose intentions are to help you to succeed, you will soon find an infinite world of wisdom and possibility exist.

CHAPTER ONE

LANDING ON MY FEET

Sometimes the greatest compliments come from the most un-expected places. I remember that day clearly. I was 19 years old, living in a small rented house with my then 6-month-old son. While I was talking to my stepsister Abbey about my future plans, she said, "Well, you know, you are someone who always somehow lands on her feet, so I'm sure you will be fine." It was an unexpected, yet strangely comforting sentiment. The idea — that perhaps, there was something unique about my approach to life which would somehow enable me to take risks, to make mis-takes, and to still be okay — was oddly profound and memorable. It was a concept I would always remember. In fact, years later I shared my story with someone about having the courage to quit my job in order to pursue the life of my dreams. This person asked, "How did you know you would land on your feet?" I smiled and thought back to that fateful day with my stepsister.

My formative years offered a very different perspective than the life I have today. My family was extremely poor. There always seemed to be a cloud hanging over us, one in which we needed to find the silver lining.

My parents were, and still are, great people who have since found relative stability. However, while I was growing up, I remember being fearful about how the bills would be paid. And I was always being reminded about how much things cost. In general, my siblings and I were taught to keep our expectations very low and that "money didn't grow on trees."

My dad was a factory worker and my mother stayed home with us until we were in school. She then went to work part time as an administrative assistant. I remember watching her get ready in the mornings and feeling proud of her as she went to work every day wearing a suit and learning new skills. Despite our struggles, my early childhood memories are of having a loving family and spending a lot of time at church nurturing a strong faith that somehow things would be okay.

My hometown was a beautiful little town at the southern tip of Lake Michigan. It was very much a blue-collar community. We lived in a small 700-square-foot, three bedroom home just up the street from the lake. It was an interesting vantage point to the rest of the world, because the majority of the houses around us were weekly vacation rentals for the wealthy Chicago families. This meant our neighbors changed weekly, and we had the benefit of getting to know each of the families as they moved in and out in a constant rotation. It was great fun and a bit of exposure to how the other half lived.

My parents divorced when I was 16 years old. It was an incredibly difficult time for me, and I went just a little wild. I was fiercely independent and also a bit boy-crazy. I ran away more times than I care to admit and got into plenty of trouble. I even dropped out of high school my junior year. I decided that driving around with boys in my 1987 Mustang convertible, which I had purchased by working after school, was more important than my studies.

At 17, I briefly took off from Indiana and headed to New York to sell products door to door. I lied to the business owners and told them I was 18. It was my first exposure to sales, and also my first opportunity to discover my own ability to be resourceful. However, after about four weeks I had enough of that lifestyle. Fortunately, I was able to come home through the Greyhound Bus Home Free program for runaways.

Upon returning home from my cross-country sales stint, I decided it was in my best interest to return to high school and finish my studies. I enrolled in a program at an alternative school intended for troublemakers like me, which enabled me to receive credit for working part time and going to school part time.

It was around then I met my future son's biological father. He was handsome and seemed sweet, and so charming. I was 17 and he was 26. I found out I was pregnant with my son Alec one week after I turned 18. My son became a powerful motivator for me, as I was driven to give him the life I felt he deserved. I consider that a pivotal point in my life and one that caused me to move in a different trajectory.

The relationship with Alec's biological father ended not long after he was born. At the age of 19, I was on my own and determined to support the two of us by any means possible. I enrolled in a community college and took a job that was strictly commissions only, which meant I had to sell. We lived in a small rented house in a safe neighborhood, and I learned how to budget.

My lowest point came when the company I worked for lost a major account and essentially went under. I lost my job, and my final payroll check even bounced. At that point, I was so broke; I could not even afford food. Shortly thereafter, I started a new sales job. I remember on the first day, I was invited by coworkers to go out to lunch with them. Unbeknownst to them, I had to decline the invitation because I could not afford to go out for lunch. I came home after that first day and remember thinking that I needed to remember what this feels like, because I had truly hit rock bottom financially. I also remember vowing to never, ever feel that way again. Fortunately, that day really was the lowest point in my life – and it is one I will never forget.

Sadly, this new job did not have the flexibility in scheduling my previous position offered, so I had to choose between college and work. I had bills to pay and a child to feed, so my education was postponed again.

My first real career opportunity came when I was hired as an admissions director for a small proprietary college that wasn't regionally accredited. At the time, I was a 20-year-old single mother with no college degree, and I had landed a job making $25,000 annually, which was great money for me – enough to make my $450 monthly rent and keep food on the table. As the admissions director, I advised other single mothers to make their education a priority and I counseled them on how to set up their life to accommodate their school schedule.

Eventually I decided I needed to take my own advice and figure out a way to continue my education, too. I researched schools in the area which offered more flexible scheduling, and I discovered Davenport University. Although the main campus was located in Grand Rapids, Michigan, I scheduled a tour of one of the regional campuses. During the admissions interview, I shared my work experience at the other school with the director of admissions. She hired me on the spot.

This new position was not only a great career opportunity for me, but it also meant I would receive tuition remission. I was able to complete my bachelor's degree, work full-time, and attend classes full-time exempt of tuition. I initially worked in the admissions office and then moved over to academic advising. As a small regional campus, most of the student population were nontraditional, first-generation college students, just like I was.

What I loved about my job was being able to meet students in the admissions process and later witness their dreams coming true as they walked across the stage in the graduation ceremony. There is something magical about being able to witness the transformation one must go through in achieving such a significant goal. I was grateful to have the opportunity to be a part of that process for the many students I was able to get to know. Each student had their own set of circumstances and their own dreams of a better life. It was my first opportunity to serve as a mentor to many of them.

I was married in 1999 when Alec was three years old. Working toward my bachelor's degree required a lot of focus and very little sleep. I worked full time. I went to school full time. And I was a wife and a mother. I remember trying to do it all. I would come home from work, pick up Alec, and get dinner on the table. Then I would do the nightly routine with him, making sure he was safely asleep in his bed before starting my studies.

I remember many nights of staying up until the wee hours of the morning while studying. I was getting perhaps two or three hours of sleep before getting up at 6 a.m. to do it all over again the next day. There were many days I wanted to give up. I was sleep deprived and weary. It was the first time in my life I felt overwhelmed much of the time. During those times, I would pause and actually envision myself walking across the stage and how I would feel on graduation day.

In 2001, my educational dreams came true when I finally did walk across the stage to receive my bachelor's degree with the highest honors. (At that time, I was four months pregnant with my daughter Paiton.) Getting my degree was a tremendous accomplishment for me. I was the first college graduate in my immediate family, and the victory was extra sweet considering the obstacles I had overcome on my way.

Not long after graduation, I left my position at the university in order to pursue a career with a large nonprofit health-related organization. I knew from my time working at the university that it was important for me to feel that my work made a difference in the lives of others, so nonprofit work was a natural choice.

While there, I discovered my love for fundraising and that I had a unique talent – I was really good at raising money! I moved up very quickly in the organization, moving from one fundraising position to another, before taking a position as a regional vice president of fundraising in 2005. This position required my family to move to Indianapolis, Indiana.

I was promoted to executive director at the age of 29. At that time, I was the youngest executive director in the country. I sometimes felt I was in way over my head, yet I had the unique benefit of working with incredible high-level volunteers who served as mentors to me.

It was my first real exposure to a different way of thinking – one of abundance and unlimited opportunity. I realized then I had a unique opportunity. While most peers in my age group were at earlier stages in their careers and contemplating starting families,

I was the executive director at a large organization and had school-aged children. I had access and relationships with some of the city's most influential people and mentors who helped me succeed. I managed a staff and regularly negotiated 6- and 7-figure deals. I knew I was very fortunate and had certainly come a long way.

Although my career was well on its way, my personal life was suffering. I filed for divorce in 2007. It is hard to say whether we were incompatible from the start or if we simply grew apart; however, it took an incredible amount of courage to acknowledge my marriage was not working and to take steps to dissolve it. It was strange to feel successful at work and a complete failure at home, but that is how I felt. In retrospect, I still had a lot to learn about love and relationships. I needed to discover my own inner happiness in order to really know what I needed within the context of a romantic relationship.

It was around that time, I started getting involved in networking groups – mainly to meet new people and develop friendships. What I found with most networking groups was they were mainly focused on business development and often catered to a certain segment of the population. I also observed the men and women within these groups tended to gravitate toward one another.

I soon got involved in a young professionals group, and I thought it would be fun to help plan a women's empowerment event. I was surprised when the women came out in droves to it. I realized then that there were other women who also had a strong desire to connect and build relationships with other energetic, successful women. I realized I had stumbled upon a need, and an idea soon blossomed.

This idea for creating a membership organization for energetic, successful women from diverse backgrounds and industries was continually growing as I reached out to other women I knew who each had a shared passion and desire to connect with other women. I pulled together an initial meeting for about eight of us to devise a plan for engaging women in our newly formed organization. The discussion centered on what we needed that did not exist at the time, and what would have been helpful to us in our own careers.

From that conversation, Mentoring Women's Network was born. Eight weeks later, our launch party had over 50 women in attendance, and the majority of them joined our group. Several months later, one of our board members created a mentoring program. We started coaching women on how to mentor effectively, the difference between mentoring and coaching, and encouraging them to share their knowledge and experience with one another in a loosely structured environment.

I had discovered my passion. Having grown up with such humble beginnings, I was influenced by my exposure to highly successful people and new ideas. I wanted women everywhere to have access to the amazing people I had the benefit of knowing.

Mentoring is powerful. Knowing what you are good at and identifying people who are experts in other areas you are weak in is what mentoring is all about. Because of Mentoring Women's Network, I essentially have my own personal board of directors and a list of people I can call on for advice in different areas. When I need marketing advice, financial advice, or even mom advice, I have a list of people I can call who excel in each of those areas. The people I call for marketing advice may be different than the people I call for mom advice, but each of their perspectives are extremely valuable.

The organization grew quickly, and it became evident it was going to require staff to keep it going. While I kept waiting for the right person to materialize and lead the organization, I felt a tug and a desire to run with it; however, I was scared. I loved my current job as executive director at the nonprofit organization and the security of knowing I had a paycheck I could count on. Building a business was not something I had experience doing, so the fear of failure was very real. As I contemplated this transition, I called on a powerful and successful mentor, a lady who had built a $50-million dollar advertising business and who also happens to be a friend and a fellow member of Mentoring Women's Network. Her response was, "Why wouldn't you?" I knew if I didn't lead the organization, I would always wonder what would have happened if I had. I did not want to reach the end of my life with this one regret.

I summoned up the courage to quit my job in order to build the organization, take it nationally, and create powerful partnerships. That same year, I was able to launch a national platform, engage some of the most powerful and influential women in our Circle 500 program, and build a virtual mentoring program. I have never looked back. My passion is helping other women connect with mentors who can serve as guideposts in their life journeys.

In my early years, I did not have access to the kind of mentors I have today. I had a lot of chaos in my life and much of it was manifested by me. Despite the chaos, I always had aspired for more. At various junctures, I had glimpses into the lives of others and was able to observe people who served as role models for me. For instance, the relationships I built with the wealthier families who inhabited the beach area in the summer taught me more about the relaxed nature and fun people can have in life when they are not burdened with constant worry.

At age 11, I also was able to visit my aunt and uncle in Switzerland for three weeks and experience the European culture. It was an incredible opportunity for me, and it taught me a world existed outside the confines of the small town I called home. This experience fostered the love of travel I have today.

When I eventually entered the workforce, I would naturally seek out the most successful people in the organization and intentionally cultivate relationships with them in order to learn from them. This alone is what I attribute much of my success to. I remember when I launched my early career in nonprofit and joined a team of fundraisers; I specifically asked my new manager what the keys were to success and who was consistently the top fundraiser. Her answer was simply "persistence," and I was able to arrange some traveling days with the top performer on the team. That individual and I became fast friends and have been friends ever since. On that same team, I quickly assessed the reason for the poor performance of the others – poor attitude and the lack of follow through. If you spend enough time with low performers, their perspective can skew your chances for success. Ensuring that the mentor you select has the right attitude and is a worthy role model is critical to the overall success of any mentoring relationship.

We often think of mentoring as an ongoing learning conversation between two individuals, but mentoring can occur in the form of simply identifying role models and observing behaviors you wish to emulate. Role models can take many forms, and by simply observing the behaviors of those around you, both good and bad, you can learn and evolve into more of the person you wish to be.

By being intentional in cultivating relationships with others who are successful or simply identifying and observing role models, you can garner the knowledge and experience of others and develop the leadership skills needed to advance your career or grow your business. You, too, can learn to lead through mentoring.

QUESTIONS:

What did you dream of being/doing/having when you were young?

_____

_____

_____

What are your dreams today?

_____

_____

_____

What are you REALLY good at?

_____

_____

_____

If you could do anything and were guaranteed success, what would it be?

_____

_____

_____

Who have been your role models?

_____

_____

_____

CHAPTER TWO

MENTORING LESSON #1: DECIDING WHAT YOU WANT PERSONALLY AND PROFESSIONALLY

I am now someone who is guided by my vision. I have willingly experienced many personal and professional changes in my life and they were all based on my vision of being equally as happy to get up and go to work in the morning as I was to go home at night. When either of those two scenarios did not apply, I was willing to make the changes necessary to fix it. Consequently, I have moved, changed jobs, and ended relationships that just did not measure up. I now know about making changes, that it all starts when you decide what it is you really want out of life.

At the age of 30, I filed for divorce from my husband at the time. That was an incredibly difficult time emotionally and I certainly do not wish that on anyone. It was necessary and important for me because it was an unfulfilling relationship and not the relationship example I wanted to set for my children. It was incredibly scary, sad, and yet liberating at the same time. I found myself back to being a single mom and uncertain about my future that was previously well defined. I decided to create a Bucket List to help me get clear on what I wanted out of life. This activity forced me to decide what I wanted and provide me with a vision to really work toward. Here is my list:

1. SKYDIVE – I completed this first in 2007, again in 2009, and again in 2011. It gets better and better each time, but I have no intent of tempting fate a fourth time.

2. GO ON VACATION BY MYSELF - I took a four day trip to San Francisco by myself in 2008.

3. WRITE A BOOK – You are currently reading the evidence of the completion of this list item.

4. GO TO TIMES SQUARE FOR NEW YEAR'S EVE – I watched the ball drop in New York City on January 1, 2008.

5. HAVE LUNCH IN ITALY – I first did this with my sister and aunt in September of 2008. We drove from my Aunt's home in Geneva, Switzerland through the Tunnel de Mont Blanc into Cor Mayeur, Italy for lunch. I have been back since and also visited Venice for further exploration.

6. SWIM WITH DOLPHINS – Checked this off in Hawaii in September 2011.

7. SEE THE GRAND CANYON – We did a helicopter tour of the Grand Canyon in November 2010.

8. GO TO HAWAII – Went to Hawaii in September 2011.

9. GO INDOOR SKYDIVING – Tried indoor skydiving in Las Vegas in November 2010.

10. SEE THE WHITE HOUSE - Was able to see the White House in 2007.

11. LEARN TO ROLLER BLADE – I learned to roller blade just after my daughter's eighth birthday in 2009. She received a pair for her birthday and we learned together.

12. SET UP A SCHOLARSHIP FUND FOR SINGLE MOTHERS – This is currently being set up through the Mentoring Women's Network Foundation.

13. KISS SOMEONE AT THE TOP OF THE STATUE OF LIBERTY – This is a list item not yet accomplished.

14. LEARN TO BARTEND – This was accomplished in January 2012. I took a bartending class and was later able to demonstrate my skills at a charity event where I donated my gratuities to my favorite charity.

15. FALL HOPELESSLY AND UNCONDITIONALLY IN LOVE – I met Jeremy in December 2011 and he has made me realize why the other relationships never worked. I cannot imagine my life without him.

16. GO TO THE SUPER BOWL - This is a list item not yet accomplished as of this writing.

17. SEE NIAGARA FALLS - This is a list item not yet accomplished as of this writing.

18. VACATION WITH MY MOTHER AND SISTER - This is a list item not yet accomplished as of this writing.

19. DO A BUNGEE JUMP – My daughter and I did this at an amusement park in 2010.

20. GO SCUBA DIVING This is a list item not yet accomplished, but on the schedule for the coming year.

21. VISIT THE EIFFEL TOWER – This was first accomplished with my Aunt in 2009 and again with Jeremy in 2013. In fact, we were in Paris when he proposed.

22. GO ON AN AFRICAN SAFARI - This is a list item not yet accomplished as of this writing.

23. WALK ON THE GREAT WALL OF CHINA - This is a list item not yet accomplished as of this writing.

24. RIDE ON THE TROLLEY IN SAN FRANCISCO – This was accomplished in 2008 when I went on vacation by myself.

25. SPEND A WHOLE DAY WATCHING OLD MOVIES IN BED – I managed to do this in 2012. I watched Casablanca, Breakfast at Tiffany's, and Gone With the Wind.

26. PLAY IN A TEXAS HOLD 'EM TOURNAMENT – This is a list item not yet accomplished. I love Texas Hold 'Em, but have not yet played in an official tournament.

27. DANCE IN THE RAIN - This is a list item not yet accomplished as of this writing. I guess I need to make it rain.

28. KISS THE BLARNEY STONE IN IRELAND - This is a list item not yet accomplished as of this writing.

29. LEARN TO GOLF - This is a list item not yet accomplished as of this writing.

30. SPEND A WHOLE DAY READING A GREAT NOVEL - This is a list item not yet accomplished as of this writing.

31. VOLUNTEER IN A SOUP KITCHEN – My kids and I did this in 2011 for the first time.

32. SLEEP UNDER THE STARS - This is a list item not yet accomplished as of this writing.

33. RENT A CABIN IN THE SMOKY MOUNTAINS - This is a list item not yet accomplished as of this writing.

34. TAKE A COOKING CLASS – I have taken a cooking demonstration class that was not what I expected and also a sushi making class. I still plan to try some sort of hands-on instructional class.

35. BECOME A CERTIFIED YOGA INSTRUCTOR - This is a list item not yet accomplished as of this writing.

36. LEARN TO BALLROOM DANCE – I took ballroom dancing with my partner at the time in early 2011. I'm not sure how much I retained, but technically did learn some things.

37. GO WHITEWATER RAFTING – I did this in 2007 with a group of friends.

38. REVISIT THE FAMILY HOME I GREW UP IN - This is a list item not yet accomplished as of this writing.

39. START MY OWN NONPROFIT – The Mentoring Women's Network Foundation was launched in 2013. Its mission is a community of empowered women developing one another personally and professionally through mentoring relationships. The Foundation also provides scholarships to women wishing to advance their skills.

40. VISIT GROUND ZERO – Did this first in January 2008 and again in July 2012.

41. RIDE IN A HOT AIR BALOON - This is a list item not yet accomplished as of this writing.

42. GET A MASTER'S DEGREE - This is a list item not yet accomplished as of this writing.

43. HAVE MY PALM READ – I did this in Nashville in November 2012. She had many interesting things to say.

44. TAKE A PHOTOGRAPHY CLASS - This is a list item not yet accomplished as of this writing.

45. RIDE A MECHANICAL BULL – I did this on my 32nd birthday. It wasn't pretty.

46. ROAD TRIP ACROSS THE COUNTRY - This is a list item not yet accomplished as of this writing.

47. FLY FIRST CLASS – I first did this in July of 2007 and again in 2009.

48. OWN A DREAM CAR - This is a list item not yet accomplished as of this writing. I do have a photo of the flashy red car I want on my vision board.

49. GROW A VEGETABLE GARDEN - This is a list item not yet accomplished as of this writing. I was not blessed with a green thumb, but am committed to make it happen.

50. TAKE A ROAD TRIP WITH A GIRLFRIEND – My childhood best friend Renee and I took a road trip to Traverse City, MI in 2008.

51. TOUR A CASTLE – My sister, aunt, and I explored a castle in Switzerland in 2008.

52. VISIT THE MALDIVES – This is a list item not yet accomplished as of this writing.

53. HAVE MY PORTRAIT PAINTED - This is a list item not yet accomplished as of this writing.

54. GO SAILING – I took a sailing lesson in 2011.

55. STAY IN A BED AND BREAKFAST – I have now done this many times, and even got married in one.

56. SING KARAOKE – I sang karaoke with my step-sister in 2000. We belted out a song by Alanis Morrisette. I feel I have done the world a favor by not returning to the karaoke mic.

57. DANCE ON STAGE - This is a list item not yet accomplished as of this writing.

58. SHOP ON RODEO DRIVE - This is a list item not yet accomplished as of this writing.

59. GO ON A CELEBRITY STAR TOUR IN HOLLYWOOD - This is a list item not yet accomplished as of this writing.

60. ATTEND A LIVE TAPING OF THE DAVID LETTERMAN SHOW - This is a list item not yet accomplished as of this writing.

61. SPEND A DAY AT THE SPA BY MYSELF – I have now done this many times. It is something I do for myself when I feel some restoration is in order.

62. TAKE A FLYING LESSON – I did this in 2009.

63. GO HORSEBACK RIDING – I did this in 2008 only to discover I am allergic to horses.

64. BE AN EXTRA IN A FILM - This is a list item not yet accomplished as of this writing.

65. MENTOR SOMEONE – Hard to believe this was on my list, but I have and will continue to mentor others, both in formal programs and otherwise.

66. RIDE A GONDOLA IN ITALY – My aunt and I rode a gondola in Venice in 2012.

67. WATCH MY DAUGHTER GET MARRIED - This is a list item not yet accomplished as of this writing. She is presently only eleven.

68. WITNESS THE BIRTH OF MY FIRST GRANDCHILD This is a list item not yet accomplished as of this writing.

69. GO TO THE MOVIE THEATER BY MYSELF – I have only done this once and it was in the afternoon on a Sunday. I watched the movie, "My Sister's Keeper" based on a book by Judith Picoult. I cried quite hard and was glad there was no one around to witness it.

70. REDECORATE MY HOUSE TO MY TASTE – In 2011, my personal life had shifted a bit and I was forced to evaluate what I wanted the next chapter to look like, so I purchased a beautiful old home which had been built in 1910. It was quite large and needed an ample amount of remodeling and decorating from top to bottom. The end result was marvelous and I did it all as a single person, which felt very good.

71. HAVE MY CAR DETAILED – I do this all the time now. There is nothing better than a freshly detailed car.

72. SPEND A YEAR TRAVELING - This is a list item not yet accomplished as of this writing. I want to spend a year living like a local, one month at a time, in exotic locations I've not yet discovered.

73. LEARN A FOREIGN LANGUAGE - This is a list item not yet accomplished as of this writing. I plan to learn French sometime soon.

74. GO ON A $1000 CLOTHING SHOPPING SPREE FOR MYSELF – In 2012, I hired an image consultant to revamp my closet and educate me on what I should and should not wear. I spent quite a bit more than $1000 that day, but it was well worth it. Prior to that, I had never spent that much on just me.

75. RUN A SUCCESSFUL BUSINESS – This had always been a dream of mine and I am proud of the businesses I now run.

76. GO ON A TOUR OF HISTORIC HOMES - This is a list item not yet accomplished as of this writing.

77. DYE MY HAIR RED This is a list item not yet accomplished as of this writing.

78. SEE A BASEBALL GAME AT FENWAY PARK - This is a list item not yet accomplished as of this writing.

79. SEE A BROADWAY SHOW IN NEW YORK – We took the kids to see a Broadway play in New York in 2012.

80. SEE DAVE MATTHEWS IN CONCERT – Got to see DMB in concert in 2010. I am a big fan of his, but not an avid concert goer.

81. GO TO THE SAN DIEGO ZOO - This is a list item not yet accomplished as of this writing.

82. SEE ALEC GRADUATE COLLEGE - This is a list item not yet accomplished as of this writing; however, he is college bound next Fall. This is a significant accomplishment because he was diagnosed with Asperger's Autism in 2004

when he was eight years old and we were told by a doctor he would never go to college. We knew then it was impossible to predict what he was capable of, and I couldn't be more proud of all he has accomplished since then. Alec is amazing and has a bright future ahead of him.

83. RESEARCH MY GENEOLOGY - This is a list item not yet accomplished.

84. BUILD A GOOD RELATIONSHIP WITH MY FATHER – My dad and I have a very good relationship now. Growing up, this simply was not the case. He is a great man.

85. AUDITION FOR A PLAY - This is a list item not yet accomplished as of this writing.

86. SEE THE EGYPTIAN PYRAMIDS - This is a list item not yet accomplished.

87. HELP SECURE A MILLION DOLLAR GIFT – I have now accomplished this many times with national partners secured for other organizations I have been involved with. My goal is to secure a gift of this nature for the Mentoring Women's Network Foundation.

88. HELP ONE OF MY EMPLOYEES GET PROMOTED – I have been able to help many employees, past and present, move into more advanced roles. There is nothing better than watching others grow and feeling like you were able to help them achieve their goals.

89. MARRY MY SOULMATE – I married the most incredible man in the world on September 21, 2013. I immediately knew he was different when we met and my world has changed for the better because of him.

90. BE A FOSTER PARENT - This is a list item not yet accomplished.

91. SEE MY NAME ON A BUILDING- This is a list item not yet accomplished.

92. THROW A HUGE PARTY AS A SINGLE PERSON – I threw a large housewarming party in December 2011 to celebrate the completion of the remodeling of my 1910 home.

93. HOST A THANKSGIVING DINNER FOR 30 - This is a list item not yet accomplished as of this writing. Thirty people is a lot.

94. TAKE A SELF-DEFENSE CLASS - This is a list item not yet accomplished as of this writing.

95. SHOOT A GUN – I shot a gun for the first time in Las Vegas in 2008 at the target shooting range at the Las Vegas Gun Shop. I used a .44 revolver. It was fun!

96. GO PARASAILING – I did this in St. Petersburg, Florida in 2009.

97. ATTEND MARDI GRAS - This is a list item not yet accomplished.

98. LEARN HOW TO RIDE A MOTORCYCLE - This is a list item not yet accomplished.

99. TAKE A SURFING LESSON - This is a list item not yet accomplished.

100. NAPA VALLEY WINE TOUR - This is a list item not yet accomplished.

As you can see, as of this writing, many of the items on the list have been completed and the two others are in the works. This list has helped me define my life, my values, and what is important to me.

Skydiving for me was an interesting way to push through the fear I had of heights. I have now gone skydiving three times and I've enjoyed it more each time. I am also happy to report I married my soul mate in 2013. I met Jeremy four years after my divorce and he is the most incredible man I have ever known. He proposed to me in Paris after a year of dating and we are excited to build a life together.

Many of the items on the list also seemed to come to me in ways I never could have imagined. For instance, I did not have an idea of what nonprofit I would launch, only that it sounded like something I would like to do. Mentoring Women's Network wasn't even an idea yet when I wrote the list. Setting up a scholarship fund for single mothers was simply a passion and my idea for wanting to help other single mothers struggling to make their way through college. When applying for nonprofit status for the Mentoring Women's Network Foundation, I was presented with the idea for awarding annual scholarships. I immediately thought about my bucket list item and became excited to have the opportunity to set this up, along with several more categories for scholarships.

Even if you think you have a vision for how you want your life to go, I highly recommend using a list to identify the experiences you want to have along the way. We each have one opportunity to go through this life and create the experiences that pleases us. It is a powerful way to create the life you want to have and will have.

If you are more visual, having a vision board is a powerful motivator as well. I have my vision board on Pinterest and it includes pictures of my future home, vehicle, vacations I intend to take, and accomplishments I will make. Whenever I want a visual of these things, I simply open up my Pinterest account and view my vision board. Others create a physical board to display in their office. In either case, this can serve as a powerful visual reminder of the life and experiences you are working towards.

If you follow this exercise to create your vision, the next step is defining what you want RIGHT NOW. What is it that you want? Are you living the life of the dreams you defined in Chapter 1? Are you ready to make some changes? It is up to you to decide! It really is that simple. Decide what you want, write it down, and create a plan for action.

On a professional level, knowing what you want is equally as important, but those plans can be more fluid and may change unexpectedly. At any given time, having a vision of what you want to be doing in 5 years is helpful in knowing what path you are on and what skills and relationships you should be developing, but having the flexibility and "Plan B" for your career is equally important as well.

An often overlooked critical success factor is being sure to build a strong network both in and outside the company. All too often I see individuals who have suddenly stepped down from their position or who found themselves downsized then realize that they haven't been taking the time to build their networks. **Waiting to build your network until you need one is way too late.** It is incredible what a strong network can do to help you navigate to your next position or opportunity. Also, having a network of others who are in similar roles can allow you to have a critical team of advisors to turn to when the challenges you are facing require different perspectives.

I look back on the time I first made it to a significant position. Short of my boss, I did not have anyone else in my life who truly understood the implications of the challenges and opportunities I was facing on a daily basis. I felt I needed to have all the answers and no one in my immediate circle had a true understanding or could offer me any insight. This is when it became critical for me to build that network and cultivate advisors I could call on.

In summation, having a vision for your life and career is essential. If you feel you are lacking vision in either area, it is good to start somewhere. Career paths can ebb and flow naturally and even the items on your vision board may change, but by taking the steps to do this, you can create the life you want to have. A strong personal and professional network of individuals who each have good perspective and are influential is also a critical success factor in shaping a successful life experience.

QUESTIONS:

What is on YOUR bucket list?

_____

_____

_____

What is it that you want in the future?

_____

_____

_____

What is it that you want RIGHT NOW?

_____

_____

_____

What does your personal network look like?

_____

_____

_____

What does your professional network look like?

_____

_____

_____

CHAPTER THREE

MENTORING LESSON #2: OWNING YOUR TALENTS

I have found many women do not openly talk about their talents. Owning what you are good at may feel like bragging, but it is incredibly liberating to truly know what your unique talents are. For some, it may be because their true talents are yet undiscovered. Perhaps, you are working in an environment where you do a decent job of what you are paid to do, yet aren't afforded the opportunity to really explore what you excel at. Perhaps you haven't found a way yet to get paid doing what you love to do. Perhaps exploring your unique talents seems a bit silly or scary.

I remember when I took the commissioned-sales job at the age of 19. Up to that point, I was actually quite shy and rather insecure. I had a deep-rooted fear of putting myself out there for fear of rejection or embarrassment. I took this job knowing I wouldn't make a dime unless I overcame my fear of selling and talking to strangers. As I was driving to work on my first day, I clearly remember coaching myself to simply do what I had to do because I had a child to feed. That was an incredible motivator.

Had I not had that experience and pushed myself, I would have continued to allow my shyness to cause me to gravitate toward jobs that didn't require me to sell. With fear as the powerful motivator, that job helped me to discover that I had a talent for selling and I quickly rose to #2 in the company in sales.

That position also turned out to be the catapult for other opportunities. By pushing myself, I discovered a true love of people and a talent for generating revenue. This talent has been the foundation for my success in the jobs I have held and in the businesses I have built. However, it takes the talent of many to create a successful business.

By recognizing the one thing I am really good at also allows me to look objectively at the MANY things I am not good at. Recognizing those areas of deficiency is the key to building a successful team. If I tried to run a business or manage a team just focusing on my talents at revenue generation, the important detail and process work would not get done. It takes all sorts of talents to make any business go.

For some, defining a true talent may not be so easy. If you have been forced to work in a profession or hone a skill that does not come naturally, you may have lost sight of your true talents. Perhaps you haven't pushed yourself to try new things because of a fear of failure or embarrassment. It would have been very easy for me to give up and go home and take a minimum wage job to support my son, but I wanted to have money to do things we enjoyed and I dreamed of a better life. Even if you don't believe in yourself, you have to push out of your comfort zone and try new things. When you discover your talent, you discover a piece of the puzzle of what you were called to do. That is where the fun really begins.

Even when the time comes that you have discovered your true talent or talents, continually pushing out of your comfort zone to try new things is fun – even if you only do to discover another thing which you are not good at. Being willing to commit to continual discovery is the spice of life. No one is truly great at everything. Owning your talent and letting others own theirs is the best way to be.

I found out that I have a natural curiosity for things. Having a natural curiosity in life enables us to intentionally push ourselves and strive to have varied life experiences. Nothing is off limits and each new frontier allows for continued growth and knowledge based on experience.

I remember the first time I went skydiving. It was one of the first things on my bucket list and an example of pushing myself to the limit because I innately have a fear of heights. I did a tandem jump and the instructions were to sit on my knees with my thumbs in my straps and let the instructor make the leap for us. Sitting in that airplane looking down 13,000 feet waiting for the instructor to make the jump was one of the most unnerving moments I can remember. When we finally did jump, the first 30-second free fall was much of a blur. Luckily, the parachute did open and we safely glided down the balance of the 6,000 or so feet. That experience helped me face my fears and open myself to new possibilities. Since that time, I am no longer as afraid of heights and continue to have natural curiosity about experiences that push beyond our limitations.

In addition to embracing having a natural curiosity and zest for life and a willingness to try new things, asking others for feedback is a great way to find out how you are perceived and what others feel are your strengths. Whether it is a formal 360 degree feedback process, or simply seeking out the input from others who work closely with you, this is a great way to learn more about the way you are perceived and what your strengths are. This personal talent assessment can offer tremendous insight on your core strengths and areas for improvement.

As an individual, it is your job to figure out what unique strengths and talents you possess and also to figure out how to offer it to the world. If you are currently working in a job you do not thoroughly enjoy, understanding what parts you hate and what parts you love will serve as clues as to what you should look for in your next opportunity or how you could potentially restructure your current position to suit your talents and energies.

Once you have a sense of what you feel are your strengths and how you are perceived by others, you can begin to hone in on those areas and seek out the expertise of others in the areas you wish to grow your skills. For instance, perhaps you'll find out you are really good at visionary leadership, but not a great team builder. This can give you a framework for identifying mentors who are strong in those areas to help you grow your knowledge base in those areas.

On the other hand, it is very easy to overuse your strengths at work by only gravitating and focusing only on the tasks you excel at and not giving enough attention to the tasks that don't hold as much interest. Think of the master chef who starts a restaurant. He or she excels at cooking and starts a restaurant in order to bring this talent to the world. However, it takes many more tasks and talents beyond cooking to make a successful restaurant go.

The same is true in business. Whether you are an entrepreneur, running a corporation, managing a team, or managing a household, being careful not to focus on one area and lose sight of the rest is critical. As a leader, your job is to teach and inspire others to learn. It is your job to be a really great teacher in the areas you excel in and hire others who have different strengths than yours to round out the team and afford you an opportunity to learn.

I think back to the really great mentors who taught me all about making the transition from an individual contributor to a leader. We are often placed in leadership roles because we excel as individual contributors. If you do not also learn the skills necessary to lead – teaching, developing, hiring great talent, inspiring others, holding others accountable, it becomes far too easy to simply continue to focus on the core strengths you honed as an individual contributor.

As an entrepreneur, this is even more critical. Anyone who has ever worked for or launched a start-up or small business knows there is a time when one has to do it all. As an entrepreneur, I have been the sales person, the accountant, the receptionist, and the janitor on any given day. When you are launching a business which requires employees, knowing how to do each job is critical to knowing the strengths and talents needed to accomplish each of the tasks.

Leading starts by owning your talents and being able to easily recognize the strengths of others. By developing your skills and helping others know and understand their personal strengths, you can grow into the kind of authentic leader you were meant to be.

QUESTIONS:

What are you really good at?

_____

_____

_____

Are you able to do what you do best every day in your current
line of work?

_____

_____

_____

How well do you spot talent?

_____

_____

_____

CHAPTER FOUR

MENTORING LESSON #3: KNOWING YOUR VALUES

Thinking about your values is one way to make sure you are living in such a way to support happiness. If your current home life or work situation does not support your unique set of values, it may be time to make some changes.

An easy way to discover your values is to think about the person in your life whom you admire the most and identify their character traits by listing them. I was asked to do this and thought immediately of my aunt, whom I am very close to and love very much. Here is my list:

- ✓ Hardworking
- ✓ Intelligent
- ✓ Insightful
- ✓ Loving
- ✓ Family-oriented
- ✓ Well-traveled
- ✓ Supportive
- ✓ Fun
- ✓ Sophisticated

After doing this activity, I was clear about my personal values. I have to work in an environment that supports these values and with people who have similar values, and my perfect mate has to encapsulate them as well.

There has been much discussion and many books written on happiness. What does it mean to be happy? Is it a reflection of our environment or a choice we actively make or both?

It is true, you have to choose to be happy, but if there are areas in your life that aren't supporting your personal values, this can present a disconnect and a life without passion that drains you of energy.

If you know your values, you can easily see if a person or situation measures up to support those values. Many people consider their list of "deal breakers" when it comes to dating, but often these are superficial. They often have to do with looks, height, money, and lifestyle habits, but have little to do with core values.

As a leader, knowing your values helps define the type of leader you wish to be, the kind of culture you should create and an environment that supports these values. I have found I often could get by in relationships or working environments that supported only some of these values, but not for very long. To be truly happy and fulfilled, all of your personal values must be supported in all areas of your life.

Creating a culture at home that supports these values is critical to your happiness. Does your spouse or significant other have shared values? What values are important to him or her? Knowing their values and life goals are often discussions that never formally take place. We like to assume everyone around us shares our values, yet they are often incongruent.

Do others who play a critical role in your life support your values? How about the culture of your organization and the members of your team? How do they measure up? What about the people who currently serve as your mentors or role models?

In addition to values, knowing what legacy you wish to leave behind is also critical. What is it you want your loved ones to say about you at your funeral? How do you wish to be remembered? It is certainly somber to think about, but this future vision can help shape you as a person and growth opportunities for becoming more of the person you wish to be.

As you are creating a vision for your life, consider a life which supports your talents and passions in an abundant fashion – one which supports your values and allows you to live out your days creating the legacy you wish to leave for your family and for the next generation. Knowing how you wish to be remembered is a powerful motivator for behaving how you wish to be in the present.

QUESTIONS:

What are your values?

_____

_____

_____

Are there areas in your life not currently supporting your values?

_____

_____

_____

If so, what changes can be made?

_____

_____

_____

How do you wish to be remembered?

_____

_____

_____

CHAPTER FIVE

MENTORING LESSON #4: HAVING COURAGE TO LET GO

What is holding you back?

It is very hard to get through this life without developing some insecurities or negative beliefs, which can hold us back from doing the things we dreamt of doing and truly living the life of our dreams. For women in particular, we are taught the importance of being pretty vs. being smart or hardworking. In so many ways, we are objectified in the media, told we are the weaker sex and discouraged from being "selfish".

I was horribly insecure for most of my life. I was shy, allowed myself to be treated poorly by others, and made many poor choices, all signifying my own inner belief that I was not good enough, smart enough, pretty enough, etc.

In my first marriage, I married a man who had some of the qualities I was looking for, but who continually looked for ways to tell me how much I didn't measure up to his standards.

Shame of my past and my own insecurities of how I was never quite good enough were what guided me at that time. I was looking for my own self-worth to be handed to me on silver platter by another human being. The people I was looking to were of my own choosing and a reflection of how I felt about myself. We teach others how to treat us and how others treat us is a reflection of how we feel about ourselves.

I firmly believe growth and happiness occur when you take a leap of faith and let go of things or situations that don't serve you. Transition is scary. It takes courage. There is no denying this. People get stuck in life time and time again because they hold onto things and situations holding them back from experiencing life the way they were meant to.

When you decide your plan is more important than what the universe is telling you and you hold on to people, situations, and material things, or simply continue doing things the way they are "supposed to" work, you are failing to evolve and learning the lesson life is trying to teach. This is true in business and this is certainly true in your professional and personal life.

When I set out to launch Mentoring Women's Network and my other business venture, Endorse Business Listings, I had a business plan and a pretty clear vision of how things were "supposed" to go. Time and time again, we tried things that absolutely did not work. Whether a failed marketing promotion or even knowing and really understanding what our value proposition really was to the world, we had so many starts and stops and frustrating failures to the point that I considered giving up many times. It took a while for me to realize these failures were simply helping us to identify what didn't work, and learning and responding quickly to what wasn't working was just as critical as uncovering what did work in all situations.

The scariest personal transition I have made was my divorce. It was sad and embarrassing and fraught with uncertainty. After 8 years of marriage, I knew the relationship was not making me happy, nor allowing me to grow, nor in line with my personal values (discussed in chapter 4). The decision was incredibly difficult and people I cared deeply about were hurt in the process. I would not wish this on anyone, yet I knew I didn't want to live my life unhappy and I also wanted to set a better example of a healthy relationship for my children, particularly my daughter. Children have a way of growing up to emulate the only example of a marital relationship they were given. The thought of my daughter being in the kind of loveless marriage which I was in was all the motivation I needed. I knew I had to take the leap of faith that the relationship I wanted and finally felt I deserved did, in fact, exist and I should be patient enough and endure enough heartache to find it.

What I found on the other side was an inner strength I didn't know I had and a real opportunity to reflect on where I went wrong. I am one hundred percent responsible for all relationships and situations in my life and my marriage was certainly no exception. I contributed equally to the demise of our marriage and we certainly tried. However, we were just and still are fundamentally incompatible. Our values are not aligned and this did not support continued growth or the happiness we both deserved.

I am certainly not advocating for divorce. I am including this as an example of the first time I was able to muster up enough courage and enough self-confidence to declare I deserved a better life. It was my first opportunity to face what I had previously viewed as a fate worse than death and learn the lessons it taught me, face my own inner demons, and emerge a stronger person because of it.

Since that time, I have made many more major transitions. I have had my heart broken, experienced many setbacks, disappointments, and betrayals. Somehow though, I am able to look back on all of these experiences and see the beauty in the lessons I have learned and the growth that has occurred. In order to truly evolve, we must let go of what is not serving us, bringing us joy, or helping us to grow. Too often, we hold on to relationships, work situations, or material things out of fear. Fear of the unknown. Fear of failure. To be willing to push through fear to experience the life of our dreams requires an incredible amount of strength, courage, and tenacity.

Through adversity, we are able to realize our own inner strength and wisdom. Through adversity, we emerge to become less afraid of the unknown and live a life with no regrets. Some of the most interesting people I have known have overcome an incredible amount of adversity in their life. Those who have done the work are able to talk about it openly. Those who haven't faced their inner demons and all of the emotions associated with them often bottle their emotions, carry the burden of shame and regret and continually subject themselves to poor decisions, whether in relationships, or with drugs and alcohol. Still, others are simply living their lives in quiet desperation, merely existing – their childhood dreams long forgotten.

I was fortunate in my line of nonprofit work to discover I had a talent and a passion for helping others. I spent 14 years working in positions I loved, yet I was somehow fascinated with those few successful entrepreneurs I knew. How could they possibly leave the security of a steady paycheck and a retirement plan? What did they know that I didn't? Where did they find their seemingly unending confidence?

When I made the decision to leave the security of a paycheck to go out into the world to follow my passion for helping women live their best lives, it took an incredible amount of courage. I had to face my fear of failure head on and acknowledge what I knew I was called to do. When I left the security of my position behind, I had no financial commitments, no guarantees, and chose to ignore the people who told me I was crazy.

However I did have the benefit of knowing some incredible mentors. Women who had achieved success and knew me well enough to tell me my plan was not crazy. I intuitively knew if I did not take the opportunity, I would spend my later years wondering if I could have made it. I would have spent my life with one regret – not taking the opportunity to follow the path of uncertainty, to really know my true grit.

Knowledge is usually acquired through the benefit of experience, but knowledge can often be attained by enlisting the wisdom of others. Calling on others who have the knowledge you are seeking because of their experience is another way to get the information you are seeking to make good decisions. This is the value of true mentoring.

Many of us only see the end result of success. We see the billionaire real estate investor, the talented and successful athletes. We kid ourselves by thinking these individuals were born lucky or with pure natural talent. What we don't see is the incredible amount of risk, sacrifice, and hard work it took to get to where they are. We don't see the setbacks and failures. We have dreams of overnight success and we long for the guarantees that all will turn out okay, that we too will somehow land on our feet.

There are no guarantees in life. However, if you are reading this book it is likely because you have a deep longing. You have been paying attention in life and know deep down what talents you have, dreams yet unrealized, and desires unfulfilled. Identifying what is holding you back is the key to unlocking your potential.

Often, when I have been filled with fear, I contemplate the worst that could happen. When faced with the unlikely scenario of the worst that could possibly happen, it often does seem to disarm the situation. Having had the benefit of experience and many setbacks, somehow the world seems less scary for me. The more you have overcome in life, the more agile you are at dealing with the unexpected happenings, and the better your problem-solving abilities become. But in order to move ahead, you first must identify what is holding you back and how willing you are to have the courage to face your fears, your insecurities, and let go of what is holding you back.

QUESTIONS:

What self-limiting beliefs hold you back?

_____

_____

_____

Are there areas in your life you could improve?

_____

_____

_____

What is preventing you from moving forward in the areas needing improvement?

_____

_____

_____

What is your greatest fear?

_____

_____

_____

What could be done to mitigate your fears?

_____

_____

_____

Who are the mentors you could call on for advice?

_____

_____

_____

Where might you find a mentor, someone who has the
knowledge from the benefit of experience?

_____

_____

_____

CHAPTER SIX

MENTORING LESSON #5: FAILURE

Failure is not a permanent condition. This is a subject I am particularly passionate about. I have the benefit of knowing a huge network of incredible women and so many of them have incredible potential and a great desire to make significant changes, yet fear of failure can be paralyzing.

We all fail. I have 'failed' at school, marriage, in business, as a parent, as a friend, as a boss, and in countless other ways. Each and every one of those 'failures' were powerful lessons about things not working the way I thought they should and helping me to identify more of the person I needed to become.

All too often, we focus on how failing made us feel, rather than focusing on the lessons failure taught us. Failing does not feel good. No one sets out to fail, yet failure is a necessary part of the learning process that goes with succeeding in any area of your life.

It is so easy to become paralyzed by a fear of failure. Change is scary because it involves breaking out of the comfort zone of the world you know and facing unknown possibilities, potential failures, and the scary proposition of realizing you have made a mistake. Even if you are in a bad situation, you can somehow find comfort in knowing what to expect.

I've been there. I know that paralyzing fear all too well and making lasting changes does not get easier, regardless of how many major transitions you end up making. Transitions in life bring forth all sorts of emotions and taking risks in life can bring on all sorts of anxiety. Your ability to tolerate anxiety is a strong predictor of how successful you will be. If you are willing to challenge yourself to achieve greater success in any area of your life, you are going to experience anxiety. If you can master the art of dealing with anxiety or learn to work well under pressure, you have a much greater chance for success in life.

Failure is a necessary part of life. If you haven't failed, you haven't pushed yourself enough. Remember the chapter on identifying your talents? Discovering what you are not good at is critical to learning more about what you have been called to do. How would I know if I wasn't good at something if I didn't attempt to do it because I was afraid of failing at it?

Life is a marathon, not a sprint. There will be obstacles. There will be setbacks. Your success is largely dependent upon your ability to start again, equipped with the lessons learned. If you aren't currently failing, you simply aren't doing enough or pushing yourself hard enough.

How often do you hear people talk about their failures when they talk about their successes? This is because they were only able to achieve success after trying multiple avenues which didn't work. They had set out with the ideal of how things were supposed to work and had enough tenacity to push ahead and start again until they finally found the path to success. How many diet success stories started by listing all of the diets and exercise programs they have tried and failed? If you really listen and understand the true success stories, they happened after many years of failing at many different things. The successful people simply have the ability to learn the lessons and start again.

I remember the one time I was fired from a job when I was in high school. I worked part-time for a real estate appraisal service briefly and came into work one day and was told I was not a good fit. Although I am still not sure specifically what indicated this, I would agree that would not have been an appropriate career path for me.

Failure is often a subject no one cares to discuss, because it is uncomfortable. Most people hold on to the image they want to project and the idea they have always had it all together and had everything figured out from day one. I assure you this was not the case for me. In fact, I can promise you I will continue to fail at many things. I will continue to make mistakes, experience setbacks, and heartaches. My goal in life is to push myself and continually strive to be my very best self and failures will be a natural part of this.

In fact, I have learned to embrace failure as a powerful lesson. We all approach life with the perspective of how things "should" work. We should be able to dance through life, meet the perfect mate, have the perfect body, and the perfect business and people should come out in droves to buy whatever it is we are selling, right? It should be easy and work exactly the way we think it should.

I believe life IS easy if you let it be. When you let go of how things "should" be and embrace the reality of how things are, you can quickly learn the lesson and adjust where necessary. This is true in business and life.

Particularly in the business world of start-ups, being able to quickly pivot is critical to survival. As a start-up, you put together a business plan and products or services you think your customer will embrace and take it to the market. The market will quickly give you feedback regarding their receptivity to what you are trying to sell.

It is critical to embrace any criticism and quickly improve or tweak where necessary, rather than holding onto the beliefs you have of how things "should" go. The great part about start-ups is the fact that making quick changes to products or strategy can generally be accomplished. It is larger companies who often can't move as quickly in response to the market.

Patience is another strong predictor of success. In my definition, patience is your ability to put forth the sustained effort over time and willingness to delay gratification to ensure the very best possible outcome. Your ability to both sustain effort and delay gratification are strong predictors of how successful you will be. This is certainly something I have struggled with over the years. We are conditioned to want everything right now – plenty of money, the perfect mate, the perfect figure, etc. We sometimes fail to enjoy the process of getting there.

Your level of impatience is also a strong predictor of success. A healthy amount of impatience with predispose you to do it now. I tend to be more impatient. I am someone who gets it done, yet I am able and willing to sustain consistent efforts toward a worthy goal. Impatience will enable you to fail faster and pivot where necessary in order to achieve your goal. Failing quickly enables you to identify what doesn't work faster, in order to identify the correct strategy more quickly. This is not always easy, but patience is the key to never, ever giving up.

One of my mentors taught me about failure and willingness to accept feedback by encouraging me to watch one of well-known talent shows. Each week, contestants compete by showcasing their talents to advance in the competition. Each week, a panel of judges shares feedback with these contestants regarding their performance. Those who are most hungry and wanting to improve will nod at the judges and thank them for their criticisms, while others will become angry. Time and time again, the winners are the ones who were able to accept the feedback and apply it to improve their next performance, while the others did not. This is a powerful example of how failure can actually propel you forward, simply by being open to the lessons it is teaching you.

QUESTIONS:

What were your most significant failures?

_____

_____

_____

What were the lessons you learned in those failures?

_____

_____

_____

What will you do differently next time because of
those lessons?

_____

_____

_____

Where are some areas you need to "fail faster"?

_____

_____

_____

Are there goals you have given up on? If so, what were the
strategies you used to try to succeed?

_____

_____

_____

List some alternative strategies to goals you have
given up on here:

_____

_____

_____

CHAPTER SEVEN

MENTORING LESSON #6: HAVING DRIVE

Successful people have several common characteristics. The foremost of these is an uncommon drive that causes them to continually push harder to achieve new heights. They are committed to continual learning and always willing to explore possibilities. They are never fully satisfied.

Successful people are not just lucky, as many people often think. They work hard. It is most often through consistent hard work and tenacity that success is realized. Although I consider myself fortunate now, I work harder than anyone I know and I have realized my own luck goes up exponentially the harder I work.

Remember the discussion on fear in Chapter 5? Fear can be an incredibly powerful motivator. When I was a young single mom, fear of not being able to pay my bills or feed my son forced me to push myself harder and ensure I was hitting the sales goals that were before me. When I left the security of my job to take Mentoring Women's Network national and also start another new business, the fear that consumed me was nearly suffocating. It is nearly impossible to describe. Pushing out of your comfort zone and stretching to new limits brings on all sorts of emotions, as discussed in Chapter 5; and harnessing and channeling these emotions is what it takes to push to new heights.

The other common characteristic is: successful people surround themselves with other successful people. You are the sum total of the 5 people you spend the most time with. The perspectives you gain from other people are based on the knowledge and wisdom they have acquired thus far. Think about it and consider those in your inner circle. What are their common characteristics? Do you consider them successful? Do they encourage you to pursue your dreams or do they make you feel foolish? Have you cultivated relationships with people you consider wildly successful? Do you even know where to begin?

Growing up the way I did, I am passionate about this topic. Although I can and do attribute many of my personality traits and strength of character to my early childhood development, it wasn't until I branched out and began cultivating relationships with successful people, that something almost magical happened. I began to develop a new perspective and a new way of thinking. I began to surround myself with people who made me feel good and had a great outlook on life – one of abundance, not scarcity. I got to know people who behaved in a way I wanted to emulate. People who were genuinely happy for me when I had an accomplishment, not threatened by it. People who made me want to be better.

I cannot over emphasize the importance of this. At the height of my own insecurity, I was surrounded by people who were battling their own inner demons and, rather than building up the people around them, chose instead to belittle them in an effort to feel better. Like attracts like, and insecure people grow up to be bullies.

It is not a fast or easy process to remove people from your life who aren't feeding your soul, drain you of energy, or just don't make you feel good, but it can be done. If the person in question is part of your everyday life, perhaps counseling may be in order. I have found simply creating some distance with certain people helps make room for others who build you up and make you feel good. Finding those people can be a challenge, but the best way is to think about the kind of people you wish to attract in your life and get involved in activities they likely take part in. Volunteering for charities, churches, or clubs are great ways to meet people who share your values and your zest for life.

Successful people have an uncommon high level of drive, passion, and also have often also cultivated a positive mental attitude. This positive mental attitude is also something that you can cultivate. Positive people absolutely attract more positive events and occurrences in their life. They are driven by an expectation of abundance and absolute joy. This positive mental attitude can be cultivated by focusing on the gratitude you have for all that surrounds you and the gifts you have been given. I keep a gratitude journal by my bedside and most nights I end the day by writing the things I am grateful for and really focusing on all of the abundance I have been given. All too often, we focus on what we don't have, and by focusing on what we don't have, it will continue to elude us.

After my divorce, I was acutely aware of what I felt I was missing in my life. I considered my divorce a failure and I am not someone who takes failure lightly. I simply wanted to run out and "fix" it. I talked about the perfect mate, prayed about it, and would look at other couples who were madly in love and feel a deep sense of jealousy. I felt it was unfair to have been handed a raw deal in the area of relationships. Everything else in my life was where I wanted it, so I focused on the one area I wanted to fix. I went on dating sites, met some very nice people (and some not so nice), and each date I went on, found myself sizing them up for future potential. I put a lot of focus on having the perfect relationship and when each did not measure up in any way, I willingly let go, though sometimes it was hard. I absolutely learned a lot in the process, but the #1 thing I learned is that if you put all of your time and energy and focus on what you don't have, it will absolutely elude you.

I finally found myself at a place where I realized all that I had. I had wonderful children, a great career, fantastic friends, a beautiful home, and I truly loved my life. I didn't need anyone to "complete" me and I finally didn't feel I needed someone else to validate who I was. I had found happiness and gratitude. That is precisely when he showed up, unexpectedly. And the rest, as they say, is history.

When it comes to success, there is no substitute for hard work, spending time with people who feed your soul, and a positive mental attitude fueled by a deep sense of gratitude. By knowing your talents, your values, your fears, and your dreams, you can channel your energies into realizing the drive it takes for success and cultivating the behaviors of those who are successful. It really is that simple.

Remember: never, ever give up.

QUESTIONS:

Who are the people in your life who feed your soul
and energize you?

_____

_____

_____

Who are the people in your life who drain you of energy?

_____

_____

_____

How will you cultivate relationships with other
successful people?

_____

_____

_____

What are you most grateful for?

_____

_____

_____

What are the ways you can demonstrate gratitude daily?

_____

_____

_____

CHAPTER EIGHT

MENTORING LESSON #7: FINDING BALANCE

Balance is a bit of a misnomer. When most women think of balance, they envision a life where everything is equal. They have just the right amount of time to do everything they need to get done. Their houses are spotless, their meals are deliciously healthy and homemade, they have plenty of quality time with their children, are able to attend every important academic or sporting event, have plenty of time for their spouse and their friends, exercise daily, have time for hobbies, and also have a fulfilling career.

Does this seem like an unattainable scenario to you? That's because it is. I have been a working mom for a long time and spent a good part of those years single. For me, work/life balance is more of a balancing act, yet is a topic that shouldn't be ignored.

The first thing we all need to realize is we shouldn't strive for perfection and will never have all of the time we would wish for to do all of the things that give us joy. I could never have enough time for my kids, there always seems to be more work to do and I have yet to figure out a way to be in two or more places at once.

What I have found is a list of priorities that seems to rotate in terms of importance. I would like to think my family priorities are always #1, but there have certainly been times when my career took precedence. I remember a time my daughter had a school play I had to miss. For Christmas, she gave me a DVD of the missed play to enable me to experience it even though I wasn't able to be there. It was incredibly thoughtful and heartwarming, yet bittersweet.

Finding balance is about figuring out what is important to you and finding a way to incorporate these activities into your life. Understanding what is important to you beyond the daily to-do lists and family/career obligations is important too.

For me, proper diet and exercise help me maintain the optimum health, clarity, and energy needed to be my best self every day for my family and for my business. When I am not eating proper whole foods and making regular time for exercise, I am sluggish, more prone to depression, and lack the clarity and focus I need to be the very best I can be.

What feeds your soul? Is it time spent with friends, reading, or exercising? For me, my family and career come first and I try to make exercise a priority, in order to be fully present and my very best self for my family and career. I like to read, but often have trouble making the time, so I resort to audio books for my long commutes in the car and ample time spent driving to meetings. And, like many of you, I don't get to spend time with my friends nearly as often as I would like, but that is to be expected.

The point of all of this is to say it is very easy to get caught up in the daily to-do lists and the mundane tasks, but having balance occurs by regularly taking the time to do the activities that feed your soul. Quality time with husband and kids, time spent with friends, and time spent doing the activities you really enjoy. Knowing what those activities are is half the battle. Having the discipline to recognize when those activities are critical is what balance is all about.

I was raised in a generation who was told we could do anything we wanted, be anything we wanted, have the family we wanted, and truly have it all. I spent much of my first marriage chasing that dream. When I was a young mother in college, I worked full-time, went to school full-time, and was a wife and mother. Like many other women, I wanted to be superwoman and prided myself on making a traditional family dinner every evening, doing the bath and nightly routine with my son, and studying only after he was fast asleep. I would often study until the wee hours of the morning and get just a few hours of sleep before getting up for work the next day.

I share that illustration because I know I am not alone. I think we, as women, put an incredible amount of pressure on ourselves and this pressure can create all sorts of anxiety and depression. I also know these issues are not gender-specific. I have talked to far too many men who wish they had spent more time with their children and I see a shift in the perspectives of the next generation of men, with many desiring to take a much more active role in their children's lives than in previous generations.

My hope is for the next generation to be far more intentional than I was in setting up my home life and establishing marital partnerships that support the couple's mutual goals. My hope is that women will learn to take care of themselves by intentionally taking part in activities that feed our soul. My hope is to inspire women to recognize they can, in fact, have a fulfilling career and a family, by setting the right intention and cutting ourselves some slack by not aspiring for unattainable goals.

Learning to let go of impossible expectations and being sure to find time for the activities that feed your soul is a powerful example to set for our children and extremely important to living your very best life.

Finding balance also includes maintaining your health. In fact, it is the #1 thing you can do for yourself and your family. It is the most important thing you can do for them. Like many, I have had my ups and downs over the years in terms of being consistent and regular with eating healthy, exercising, and abstaining from any unhealthy substances. What I have found, however, is that changed habits occur through sustained effort. By developing those habits, I find that I naturally select healthier foods and on Sunday evenings, I schedule my workouts to try to fit them in. My schedule is varied and the only way I get exercise in is by creating the intention.

Many diets are based on scarcity – you can't have this, you shouldn't have that. When you operate from a mentality of scarcity when it comes to food, it promotes deprivation. When I switched to a focus on what I can and should have - the wonderful whole fruits, vegetables, and proteins that we are fortunate enough to have in abundance, it all suddenly clicked for me.

Aside from the physical benefits of taking good care of ourselves, the mental clarity, energy, and stamina that results directly translates to productivity at work. Attitude improves, relationships improve, and creativity is free to flow.

Doing the best we can, without judgment, to take care of ourselves and feed our souls outside of work enables us to lead more effectively. Knowing what feeds us and being sure to incorporate what is most important to us into our routines is the key to living a happy, vibrant life – and a powerful example to set for the next generation.

QUESTIONS:

What are the obligations and responsibilities you
currently balance?

_____

_____

_____

What are the regular activities you personally need
to restore YOU?

_____

_____

_____

How might you adjust your routine to ensure you are regularly
being restored?

_____

_____

_____

What guilt should you be letting go of?

_____

_____

_____

What are the ways you can improve or maintain your health?

_____

_____

_____

CHAPTER NINE

MENTORING LESSON #8: CREATING A VISION AND MAKING IT A REALITY

So now you have thought about your talents, your dreams and defined what you want and what is holding you back. You have considered your values and identified what feeds your soul. Now is where the true fun begins.

What is your vision? Different from your goals, what is the vision for the life that you want?

Until fairly recently, my vision was quite simple:

"To be as excited to get up in the morning to go to work as I was to go home at night."

In other words, I longed for the kind of career and line of work that I was excited to go to each day and the life partner and family situation which would bring me a sense of joy and excitement that made it fun to go home at night. That simple vision was what guided me towards the life I now have.

My life vision has evolved a bit:

> "To be excited to get up in the morning and have the ability to do what I do best every day. To do work that is meaningful and has a lasting impact. To follow my passion for helping others and making the world a better place.
>
> To grow and evolve with my husband around a shared sense of values and to be the kind of mother who cultivates her children into young adults who are intent on living their best lives.
>
> To leave a legacy behind. A legacy of a culture of women supporting one another through mentoring relationships. I hope to be remembered for my hard work, my vision, my love of people, and my contributions to society. I hope people will remember me as generous, funny, and a great mom, spouse, sister, daughter, and friend. Above all, I hope to be remembered for leaving the world just a little better than I found it."

That is my vision. It incorporates all of the items we have discussed so far. Knowing what you want, owning your talents, defining your values and thinking about your legacy all lead to the creation of your vision.

What is your vision? What is it you dare to dream? What is so all-encompassing and inspiring to you in the here and now that supports the legacy you wish to create?

To create your own vision, start with what you want right now. What, if anything, do you wish to change? Are you as excited to get up in the morning to go to work as you are to go home at night? If so, that is a great start. If not, what needs to change?

Can you take your vision further than that? What is the legacy you wish to leave behind? How do you wish to be remembered? These are powerful concepts to entertain and worth revisiting over and over again.

Great leaders have great vision for themselves, the life they wish to create, and the companies they are contributing to. The key to making your vision a reality is backing it up with the tactical strategies to make it happen.

Great vision is what is needed to identify the path from here to there, but remember that simply having a vision alone will not get you there. How many dreamers do you know? Dreamers are dreamers because they have great vision, but lack any steps or follow through to get there. Life is truly easy if you allow it to be.

If you have made it this far and completed the exercises, you have defined your values and identified your strengths. You have identified what is currently holding you back and have thought about your fears. Perhaps you are already living the life of your dreams and if so, you still have an opportunity to take your dreams one step further, to stretch your reality.

What is your vision? What have you been called to do and what can you contribute to the world? What does living a happy, vibrant life mean to you? Where do you see yourself financially? So many people live their lives in quiet desperation and are afraid to embrace the life they were called to live. Please, do not let that be you! You owe it to the world to do what you have been called to do and live the life of your dreams. The world needs you!

My personal vision now is to travel the world and live like a local, a month at a time, in exotic places. My vision is to have the financial flexibility to be able to accomplish this and a business that supports the ability to travel extensively. I know this will happen and have a plan for making it so.

The legacy I wish to leave is to be a leader who inspired others to live their best life and be open to possibility. I also wish to be remembered as a great mom, wife, sister, daughter, and friend. To leave this world knowing I made it just a little bit better, through my work and contributions to society.

I have a vision the world of work will be a very different place for my daughter. She will have equal opportunity and will not feel compelled to choose between her dreams. She will be well-supported in the workplace and value herself personally and professionally. The gender and minority balance in the C-Suite will be reflective of the society in which we live. To achieve this vision will take great strength and sustained effort on the part of many. To achieve this vision, we need you.

QUESTIONS:

What is your personal vision?

_____

_____

_____

What have you been called to do?

_____

_____

_____

What do you dream of having/doing/being?

_____

_____

_____

What do you want your legacy to be?

_____

_____

_____

What is the daring thing you have been afraid to do?

_____

_____

_____

C H A P T E R   T E N

HARNESSING THE
POWER OF MENTORING

I met my first true mentor in every sense of the word when I was 25 years old. For a year and a half, I had worked in my first entry-level position and I wanted to move up in the organization. A Regional Vice President role became available in another state and another department, for which I was wholly unqualified for, and I applied. I did all the politically appropriate things in the process – I notified my current supervisor of my intent and did everything I could to prepare for this interview to truly go for it, despite my lack of experience.

I drove four hours to that interview and met a woman who would later become instrumental in my career. In retrospect, I am pretty sure she granted the interview to simply meet the girl who had the chutzpah to apply for such an advanced position. She did not offer me that particular position, but did come back to offer me a lateral position and explained to me it would allow me to build the experience I needed to really be considered when the next opportunity became available. It also gave me an opportunity to work under her and learn from her.

Six months later, a similar position did open and I was hired to be a Regional Vice President and went on to become Executive Director a short time after that. In fact, I remember the day I became Executive Director. I was not even thirty yet. The morning arrived and my very first meeting was a board room full of men at least twenty years my senior and I had to speak with authority and vision for the organization I served. She was right there to coach me and prepare me to assume my authority.

She taught me a lot. She was always willing to give me feedback even when it was tough and she served as a sponsor for me. She certainly didn't pull any punches and taught me to boldly lead as an authentic female leader, despite my young age. The fact she was a woman helped me to navigate the sometimes difficult situations that I had to face. She helped guide me by sharing her perspectives on managing staff situations and work/life balance issues, and was supportive through my divorce. I was able to observe her behavior and model the ones I wished to emulate.

In my role as a non-profit Executive Director, I also had the unique opportunity to have access to some of the city's most influential leaders. I had the benefit of working with the top CEOs on various fundraising events and cultivate relationships with many incredibly intelligent, strategic and passionate people who also served as mentors for me. Each were critical in my development and their perspectives helped shape me into more of the kind of leader I wished to become. I realized quickly I was incredibly fortunate to have relationships with such wonderful and influential people and I wanted others to have that opportunity. That is how Mentoring Women's Network was started. I pulled together eight women who had a shared passion for inspiring and empowering women and we each shared our stories about how mentoring played such a critical role in our own development and wanted to create a venue for women coming together to help inspire and develop one another.

Since that time, I have broadened my network to include many more wonderful individuals who serve as mentors to me. Each person in my life brings their own unique talents, skill sets, and perspectives. I have a list of people I can call for business and financial advice; I have a list of people I can call for parenting advice - and everything in between. I have also gotten really clear on my own personal competencies and regularly share my knowledge and experience, both formally through our mentoring program, and informally in my ongoing relationships with others.

Mentoring is defined as a type of knowledge transfer. Intentionally seeking out the knowledge and wisdom of others who have been successful in the area of knowledge you are seeking is better than any other formal education you could seek out.

Think about who you are currently seeking advice from. Are they successful themselves in the area they are sharing advice about? Are they broke, but giving you advice about money? Are they terrible parents and telling you how you should parent? Thinking critically about who you are getting advice from and their own levels of success cannot be overstated. Mentoring should occur from the perspective of experience. If the person giving you advice has not been successful in the area they are giving you counsel or operating from a negative perspective, my advice is to seek out successful people who do have the wisdom you are seeking.

A personal example of this phenomenon occurred when I was single looking for my life partner. Time and time again, I was told what I was looking for "didn't exist" and I needed to learn to "take the good with the bad". I was told I was too picky and no one could possibly meet my high standards. Yet, when I looked critically at those who were giving me this advice, I saw they were speaking from their own life experiences. They hadn't experienced the kind of fulfilling, harmonious, and loving relationship I was seeking and therefore, made the incorrect assumption it didn't exist. Many people do settle in this area. Holding out for the right one or making a change when necessary can be excruciating and requires a whole lot of faith and a whole lot of courage. Yet, seeking advice from those who are involved in the kind of relationship you wish to have, rather than those who have never experienced what you are seeking is a powerful example of cultivating mentoring relationships with those who are operating from a knowledge base acquired by experience.

Here are some qualities to look for in a mentor:

Compassion – Do they look at others with a sense of understanding and true caring?

Integrity – Do they live the values they subscribe to, or do they behave one way publicly and an entirely different way when they think no one is looking?

Leadership – Do they inspire you to be a better person?

Empathy – Do they seem to understand where you are coming from and approach things from your perspective?

Openness/Candor – Are they warm and open and willing to be candid with you and give you the feedback needed to help you grow?

Empowerment – Do they empower others to do their very best or do they control every detail for those around them?

Commitment – Do they follow through and always do what they say they will do?

Passion – Do they have a zest for life and light up when they talk about what they are most interested in?

Honesty – Are they truthful and consistently demonstrate integrity?

Energy/Excitement – Do they have a passion and a zest for life and demonstrate an excitement about the topic you are wanting to learn from them?

Friendliness – Are they warm and approachable?

Communication – Do they communicate in such a way that is easily understood and also makes you feel understood?

Lifelong Learner – Do they seek out new information or ways of doing things? Are they open to new ideas?

Follow Through – Do they finish what they start or are they all talk?

Demonstrated Success – Do they have a strong track record?

Self Awareness – No one is perfect. Do they seem to have a sense of who they are, how others see them, and areas of strengths and weakness?

Intentionally seeking out mentors who have those qualities and true experience in the competency you are hoping to develop is a powerful way to develop the skills you need to go to the next level – whether this is in your corporate career, your business, or in life. The benefits of mentoring cannot be overstated, and mentoring is not a one-way street. I find I learn just as much from my mentee as they are learning from me. I gain a better understanding of the challenges facing the next generation and sharpen my own communication and problem-solving abilities.

As a leader, modeling a mentality of knowledge sharing and transfer in the form of mentoring is a powerful way to build a culture for your company or your network. A mentoring program is a wonderful way to build a culture of sharing and building. This is perhaps the best way to really capitalize on the strengths of the team.

At Mentoring Women's Network, we offer access to mentors through our network of ambitious, successful, smart, and driven women. We have created a novel approach to a mentoring program, matching based on competencies and experience levels, and accomplished through a virtual nationwide network of women leaders sharing and developing one another through mentoring relationships.

We counsel our members on what qualities to look for in a mentor and also work to help them identify what qualities in a mentor would be helpful to them in the stage of their lives they are in. Our mentoring program is based on the transfer of knowledge that occurs through the exchange of conversations between mentor and mentee. We train both mentors and mentees on what to expect from the relationship and give a broad understanding of what mentoring is. Our broad network affords mentoring from an external perspective, often from women in different industries. Our members come together to support one another personally and professionally in a caring environment. Our aim is to help women advance in the workplace and achieve their leadership potential.

In the traditional model of a company-sponsored mentoring program, mentoring is an ongoing relationship where mentors and mentees meet face to face once a month in an often forced relationship with no clearly defined goals. Many companies do not incorporate training into their mentoring program to help both mentors and mentees understand the context of the relationship and what is being asked of them. We offer resources to companies wishing to set up or enhance their mentoring program to aid in the success of the overall program.

Our own mentoring program was based on the idea that mentoring occurs by cultivating relationships with those who have the knowledge you are seeking and being able to call on them from time to time for advice. I have many great mentors in my life whom I call on from time to time when I need them, without the burden of a set schedule at regular intervals. It is a relationship and checking in regularly in-person or otherwise, should simply occur naturally.

I keep in touch with all of my mentors, including some of my former bosses (the ones I consider mentors) this way. Every so often or when I am facing something I want to bounce off of someone, I call upon the people I know who have experience with the challenges I am facing. For me, cultivating mentors has opened up a world of possibility. It is like having my own personal board of directors, all intent on helping me achieve my greatest potential. It is really amazing to have this level of support.

Additionally, mentoring others formally and informally is critical to inspiring the next generation. I often speak to people who identify their children or employees as their only mentees. Children and employees are going to learn from you no matter what, and although it is important to serve as a mentor for them, I am challenging you to think outside of that box. Who are you mentoring and how are you seeking out those relationships?

Often, we get so consumed by our day to day lives that we don't stop and think about how we are truly inspiring the next generation. Many mentoring programs require a time commitment or logistics that won't work for our busy schedules. I am challenging you to commit to intentionally seeking out ways to share your knowledge and experience with others in an intentional and meaningful way. I feel it is a calling we each have, to inspire the next generation. You could write a book or host a seminar to share your knowledge with larger groups, or you could sign up for a mentoring program to teach and educate the next generation.

I have a particular passion for advancing young women. Young girls are subjected to so many things at an early age which have a way of negatively impacting their self-esteem. We are taught to value our exterior image far more than our intelligence. Whether it is the media messages or the impact of being raised by mothers who have their own issues resulting from years of not being made to feel good enough, it is no wonder so many are subject to eating disorders, self-esteem issues, and toleration of abuse from others. This cycle needs to stop and, for those of us fortunate enough to have begun to break that cycle, we have a social responsibility to the next generation to educate, develop, and empower them to know their value and their worth and grow to be the very best they can be.

Relationships such as this do not have to be formal and they do not have to start by telling someone you would like to mentor them. They start by intentionally seeking out those who are struggling in areas you have learned to excel in and beginning to mentor them by suggesting some tools and resources which may help them in their journey. Simply taking notice and an interest in others can have a profound impact on someone.

Our mentoring program requires our executives and entrepreneurs to give us one hour per month. One hour per month to change someone's life. We have a diverse population of women from a variety of backgrounds and financial circumstances, all coming together to support one another, and it starts with an hour per month.

If you are like me and have a passion for helping others, you will be amazed with the impact you can have and the pride you will feel when you know you have made a difference in the life of your mentee by the success they attain because you cared enough to spend time listening to them and giving them advice. You'll also be amazed with what you get in return.

CHAPTER ELEVEN

NEEDED:
MORE WOMEN LEADERS

In my role as President and CEO of Mentoring Women's Network, I regularly consult organizations on the need to advance women leaders. I get to talk to companies about their wonderful leadership initiatives and watch the color drain from their faces when I ask about the gender composition of the Senior Management Team. All too often, that number is twenty percent or less. In fact, they are often proud when they report a number higher than thirty percent, which is ironic, since women make up more than half of the population.

In 2011, women were paid 77 cents for every dollar a man made and many organizations are seeing a huge gender gap between the middle management level and the executive suite.

I was raised in the generation of women who were told you can absolutely have it all, be anything you wanted to be, and balance it all with a family. I was made to believe I could one day be president. Yet the statistics tell a very different story.

We still have to fight twice as hard for opportunities and find a way to address these disparities. I believe the work we do at Mentoring Women's Network with corporations to align strategies to support the advancement of women is so critically necessary, and there is much work to be done.

I remember the time I spoke to my supervisor about the promotion I wanted to be recommended for and he discouraged me from applying because I "had a family to think about". Yet the majority of his Senior Management Team were men who also had children.

I have heard many of these similar types of stories with very common themes of powerful assumptions made about women in their careers based on their current or potential future family considerations. Many of these assumptions are well-intentioned, but certainly have a way of holding us back from realizing our leadership potential. I have also been told by many executives they have come to expect women to lose momentum after one child and leave altogether after two. When organizations operate with this assumption, it tends to become a self-fulfilling prophecy.

The statistics related to women entrepreneurs is even worse. Female entrepreneurs pay themselves, on average, only 51 cents for every dollar a man makes and she faces less favorable considerations when it comes to getting funded for her business than men. (Source: 2010 US Department of Economics and Statistics Information for the White House Council on Women and Girls.)

All of these statistics support the reason Mentoring Women's Network exists. I am passionate about the need for women to stop living lives of quiet desperation, own their talents and their passions, make a plan and GO FOR IT!

Finding mentors and building a personal board of directors who are there to provide guidance and support is one key to the strategy of building a life of your dreams. I cannot emphasize this enough. Being a part of Mentoring Women's Network and cultivating relationships with other successful, energetic, powerful, supportive women has opened more doors for me than I ever could have imagined.

In addition, building initiatives and programs aimed at advancing women leaders is critical. We have a true opportunity to teach women to lead authentically and fearlessly, to seek out mentors, cultivate sponsors, and mentor and sponsor others. The statistics related to this topic are alarming and we have so much work to do.

On a very basic and fundamental level, building a community of empowered women developing one another personally and professionally through mentoring relationships has created an amazing culture of women all intent on helping to support one another personally and professionally. Our hope is this culture will transcend into the workplace and we will begin to willingly help one another advance, rather than viewing one another competitively. By rising up, owning our strengths and talents and creating a vision, we will achieve success beyond measure and pave the way for our daughters' opportunities in the future and set a powerful example for them.

At Mentoring Women's Network, we have programs and strategies which align support towards the advancement of women leaders within companies. Our Project Lead program is a one year program broken into four modules designed for more senior leaders and covers such topics as talent management, succession planning, and being intentional in sponsoring and being sponsored for advanced positions. Our Emerging Leaders program is designed for women who are at a management level and above to work on skill development for the soft skills of leadership, as well as access to our virtual mentoring program.

These programs, along with the virtual mentoring program and nationwide access to other high energy, successful, ambitious, and driven women throughout the country, create the intentional strategies and support needed to afford women the skills and resources necessary to advance in the workplace.

We believe the advancement of women leaders can be accomplished with intention and the access to powerful mentors who can serve as guideposts along the way.

To learn more about personal membership, consulting services, our virtual mentoring program, and mentoring software, visit **www.mentoringwomensnetwork.com** today.

C H A P T E R T W E L V E

STORIES OF
INSPIRING MENTORS

The following are excerpts of stories shared from other female leaders on the impact mentoring has had on their life and their career:

TONJA EAGAN

CEO, The Leadership Institute – Women With Purpose

At last, I made it to the fall semester of my undergraduate senior year of college (August 1989). It had been a long haul and a struggle for me working full-time, while attending college full-time, and dealing with the drama of life along the way. Many times I lost hope that it was worth the emotional and financial sacrifice and investment to complete a college education. I was motivated by the fear of what life would be if I did not earn a degree to support my career. I was not feeling inspired, I was tired.

As my senior capstone course, *Society and Racism,* began we were excited to learn we were part of a new pilot project for students to use email as a form of communication with their instructors (yes, email in the classroom was a novelty in 1989). Because of this unique pilot and the impact the email experience could have on the future of college education, one of our instructors was the Vice Chancellor for Undergraduate Affairs, Dr. J. Herman Blake. To me, this meant nothing other than I was going to try out something new and use email to talk to my instructor.

During our first on-line assignment, we shared our own personal stories of racial discrimination. As a Caucasian woman, I did not feel that I had much to contribute, but my instructor encouraged me to delve deep into my emotions and experiences and think of how discrimination against others in my community had impacted me. His words of encouragement through our many email exchanges were unlike other professors, as I felt a sense that he really wanted me to grow through this educational experience. For the first few weeks of class, we only communicated via email, but for me I had a connection to him that I had not previously experienced. He made me feel that I was not only a valuable contributor to the course, but that I even had my own special purpose for being on earth! Internally, I began to feel inspired as though there was hope for a bright future for me.

The second month of class, which was our first day to meet in person, I sat there eager to meet the "mystery man," who seemed to understand me and care about my well-being as a student. I was a Caucasian middle-class woman, age 22, waist-length blonde hair, who had learned to get by with life on my looks more than my smarts. Into the classroom walked a middle-aged, heavy-set African American man in a suit. I thought to myself, "who is he?" Then, he introduced himself in a robust voice as Dr. J. Herman Blake. As my jaw dropped, I nearly slid out of my seat. This is the man I could relate so well to via email? What on earth did *he* have in common with *me*? We looked as though we were from two opposite ends of life's spectrum!

Dr. Blake had a strong sense of self that I admired. He had a genuine care and concern for all the students in the course, and yet he still had a way of making me feel as though I had something special to offer as a person and as a young woman. Over the course of the semester, he challenged me, praised me, and seemed as intrigued by my life experiences, as I was by his. He helped me see assets within myself that I never knew existed. I caught myself talking with friends and family about my future and even attending graduate school. No one could believe I was open to more formal education since I had lamented for five years how eager I was to graduate and never look back! I learned to expect more of myself, in large part because Dr. Blake had high expectations for me.

At my May 1990 graduation ceremony, Dr. J. Herman Blake approached me. He asked me what I planned to do next. As a 23 year-old sociology major and recent graduate, I was asking myself that very same question. He then offered me a full-time position within the university as the founding Director of the Student Mentor Program. When I asked why me, he said that I had a keen sense of awareness of the needs of commuter students who worked and attended school full-time. He said I had a strong work ethic and I was motivated to change the commuter campus community to create a sense of community for all students. Well, he was right!

For four years I worked under his tutelage as my boss. For the first three weeks on the job I awaited his instruction as to how I was to build a Student Mentor Program on a campus of 19,000 students. He told me to first look for best practices and do a literature review on student mentoring. Then, he said, build a plan and implement it. That is when it struck me that he expected *me* to take the lead, and that he is not going to hold my hand every step of the way; rather would have my back and offer advice as needed. It was surreal to realize how much he was investing in me and my ability to build a new mentoring program for students. He had faith in me, which gave me the confidence to proceed.

There were bumps on the road, and I recall running to his office one day in tears because I felt disrespected by some tenured Ph.D. faculty who saw little value in my opinion as someone with only an undergraduate degree. I explained that because I was a woman in my early 20's no one respected or valued me as a professional. Dr. Blake looked directly into my eyes and said, *"That is not your problem! Those are their issues so quit making their issues your problem."* He told me to quit seeking nay-sayers and find the true believers who want to transform the student experience at the university and work with them. The nay-sayers will come once they see success. He also told me to stop asking for permission and realize that it is much easier to succeed if I seek forgiveness rather than permission. Being willing to take risks, fail and admit fault a few times is the best way to succeed -- not to try and win over everyone and seek their approval and permission every step of the way. He would always end our discussions by saying, *"Keep on keeping on."*

Over the course of five years, we had many conversations that changed my perspective on life. In the five years that Dr. Blake was directly involved in my life as a mentor, I never once realized he was my mentor. It was not until my late 20's that I began realizing how much of the lessons he taught me were imbedded in so many of my thoughts and actions as a leader in my professional and personal life. It was not until people started asking me who mentored me that I began sharing the impact Dr. Blake had on my life. I also cautioned people to realize that had someone asked me at age 22 to identify and select a mentor, I probably would have chosen a woman who looked and acted similar to me. After all, that was my comfort zone. There is great opportunity in having a mentor who is uniquely different than ourselves and who can help hold a mirror up for us to see ourselves from a new perspective.

Nearly 20 years has passed since the time Dr. Blake and I worked together, and we lost contact along the way. I often thought of him and his wisdom and recently was sharing with a woman the impact he had on me. Ironically, she knew him and sent him my contact information. Just two weeks ago, I received the following email from him and as I read it, I felt that same sense of pride and feelings of confidence and empowerment that he always gave me.

> Dear Tonja:
> I was thrilled to receive the news about your new position and The Leadership Institute. Your intuitive insights, your wide-ranging experiences, as well as your intellectual skills are a rare combination. You have so much to offer. Do well.
>
> Keep on keeping on.
> J. Herman Blake, PhD

In essence, I realized that once a mentor, always a mentor. I am forever grateful to the man and mentor who made me the woman I am today. I devote much of my time to mentoring others, especially girls and women, because I know firsthand that mentoring can transform a life. Yes indeed, Dr. Blake, thanks to your mentorship, I will *"Keep on keeping on."*

MELISSA GREENWELL

Chief Human Resources Officer, Finish Line, Inc

It was a man's world from the very beginning. I grew up one of seven children, with five brothers and a sister, a domineering father and a very patient mother. I quickly understood the nature of competition in a male-dominated environment. As the oldest daughter, I did not get recognition from my father for babysitting, cooking, dishes or getting kids off to school, but only for the occasions when I was able to fix something mechanical, like a mower or my own car.

My family had limited resources. Neither of my parents had a college education, nor came from families that did have one. When I was in my senior year of high school, I started talking to my parents about going to college. Their response was that they did not have the resources to help me. If I were to go, I'd have to figure out how to accomplish that on my own. While I was a good student, I did not know how to navigate the system of financial aid. When I complained or verbally worried about the situation with my mother, she would say, *"You'll figure it out,"* and *"There's nothing stopping you."* At that moment, she became my first mentor. Over and over again I watched her overcome great obstacles because of her quiet determination and that she was teaching me to do the same. I graduated from high school, got a job and started saving.

My first job was as a "secretary," as they used to refer to it, in a law firm. I took evening classes at the local community college when I could. My second job was at a car dealership, thanks to an observant client of the law firm who thought my customer service skills would be useful. He was my second mentor. He taught me about the product, made me take quizzes and role-played customer conversations. I continued to pursue my education one class at a time. My third job was with a large manufacturing company that had a very generous tuition reimbursement program. I was approved for the program and finally was able to make some real traction on my education. All along the way, my professional responsibilities grew and were always contingent upon me finishing my education. I completed my undergrad the month I turned 30.

I was fortunate that so many people took an interest in my development early in my career. All of them were men. They took the time to give me career advice, teach me about a certain business, and provide me with stretch opportunities and encouragement. They saw potential, talked about the possibilities and this gave me the confidence I needed to dream. I wish I could say that one particular individual stood out, but when I think about it, I had at least seven.

Therein lays an important point. I did not have the opportunity to work for a strong female leader until later in my career. That was a whole new learning curve for me. I learned to navigate a relationship with female leadership differently -- less chit chat, more facts, more logic, less emotion, less raising of voices and more caring about how people were treated. For me, mentoring had come full circle, relating back to what my mother had taught me. First, be a good person; always do the right thing. Doing the right thing trumps any other consideration. Gather the facts, analyze the situation, create a plan of attack, and adjust when necessary. In short, figure it out!

Lots of people can be good mentors, men and women alike. We need both, in fact, because men and women offer different perspectives. Unfortunately, with roadblocks – some imposed, some self-imposed- we still see a shortage of women in senior leadership positions in many industries and government. I encourage women to stop and ask themselves the same question my mother asked me: *"What's stopping you?"*

Women often don't pursue stretch opportunities because we think we have to know 100% before we take it on, or that we have to make great personal sacrifices that impact our families. Is that really true? I offer to say that it is not.

Today, I realized my desire and responsibility to mentor other women early in their careers. No magical number of years of age or experience makes you a good leader, it's the experiences you have and what you learn from them. I hope to share my experiences and learning in a way that helps other women accelerate their path to leadership opportunities.

NICOLE GEBHARDT

President, Geb*Art Strategic Communications

I wanted to work in corporate America ever since I saw the previews for the movie "9 to 5" in the early 1980's. I was too young to watch the movie, but for some reason I became enamored with the idea of wearing a nice skirt suit, pantyhose, and tennis shoes after a day battling paperwork in high heels. Perhaps that's why my first business mentor was the epitome of the woman I wanted to be.

I was just a 20-year old intern when I started working at Caterpillar Inc. 'Carolyn' was THE woman I wanted to be. Courageous and strong, savvy and stylish, she could hold her own at any conference table in our male-dominated manufacturing environment. For many of the 12 years of my career there, she was the highest ranking woman in the office and she was my mentor. Occasionally, she was my boss as we both moved up the ranks.

It's not an easy task to rise up in such an environment. It was Carolyn who taught me the artful balance of beauty and beast.

"Never bring in foods you've baked," she advised. *"They'll perceive you to be like their wife."*

I learned to bring donuts.

"Sit. Wait. Don't be the first to jump if something needs done."

I learned to behave as their equal.

"Dress sharp with a touch of femininity. Splurge on the important pieces."

I learned the art of personal branding.

From the basics of shopping to art of commanding attention in a meeting, she took me under her wing like a daughter. She candidly shared her mistakes.

I imagine there were times she cried after work, perhaps out of frustration, (I did) but I never saw her flinch at the office. She responded with grace, diligence and determination and taught me to do the same.

"Today will pass. Keep your eye on the long-term."

Eventually we both traded in our high heels for tennis shoes. Carolyn retired to travel, and I chose motherhood for a few years before starting my own coaching business. I know I owe much of my success today, as I did then, to her mentoring.

TIFFANY OLSON

President and General Manager, Nuclear Pharmacy Services, Cardinal Health

Throughout my career, I have had several mentors that have helped in my professional and personal growth. They have been men and women both internal and external to my organizations. The relationships have been both formal and informal, but none is as important as my first mentor; my mother.

My mother was a working woman back when very few mothers worked full-time outside of the home. Being a single parent who worked in human resources for General Mills, she was very familiar with the many challenges women encounter in business.

As I was graduating from college and deciding what to do with my career, her advice and counsel are something I have used over and over again and also have been reinforced by my many other mentors.

As a graduation gift, my mother gave me a book. Many of my friends were receiving money, trips and even cars, so a book didn't seem too exciting or important at the time. Written ironically by a man (John T. Molloy), "The Woman's Dress For Success Book" was about appropriate fashion for business women in the 70s and 80s. Similar to a cook book, it reviewed the dos and don'ts of dressing for the office if you wanted to get ahead in your career. It had illustrations and advice for women, such as, too curly hair tested poorly for the business woman (page 85) and never wear a pinstriped or chalk-striped suit. Along with the book, my mom's gift included taking me shopping for my first business wardrobe. Shopping with my mother is not for the faint of heart as 'shop until you drop' is her personal motto.

But the fact she was going to be paying for clothes eased my pain.

We were soon off to the mall. We walked into the mall with my mentor/mother holding the book like the Archbishop holds the Bible walking into Mass. As we entered the mall, my mother proclaimed, "My daughter needs to be dressed." She then turned to page 29 of the book and we proceeded with shopping.

Five hours later and after several packages of "appropriate" business attire, we were ready to go home. It was as we were walking to the car that my mom shared with me the real gift - as her wisdom and advice was not about what to wear on the outside but also what to wear on the inside. She told me, *"No matter what the season — make sure you're wearing your self-confidence and integrity."* Her advice: dress yourself starting from the inside first.

This advice from my first mentor has never failed me. When I'm challenged in business, I know that if I bring confidence in my knowledge and experience combined with integrity, I can't go wrong. This has been especially true as I have moved up in my career. The values that you bring as a leader creates the foundation of the culture you create. Integrity can become a vital and important part of your company's culture and your personal brand - you must always wear it to work.

SHERI ALEXANDER

Senior Vice President, Employee Division Manager, Gregory and Appel Insurance

I have been blessed to have several mentors during my 30+ year career and each has played a key role in my personal and professional development. I was 21 years old when Carol, my first mentor, coaxed me into the insurance industry and began to continually remind me that I could do anything I put my mind to. She knew I would eventually move on to bigger and better things but she was unwavering in her support for the nine years we worked together. My second mentor, Gene, was a seasoned and scrappy guy who called me his "diamond in the rough". He plucked me from the comfort of my first employer and steered me toward sales. Mind you, I was convinced I had no sales skills whatsoever. Under his guidance, my career took off and I went on to lead our national division in sales two years in a row. Talk about insight. Gene taught me how to lead, look for the best in others, be patient, and appreciate that "less is more". I know first- hand how valuable a mentor can be and also have spent the last several years mentoring many men and women in our industry. If I can have a fraction of the positive influence on them that my mentors have had on me, then I will have done well.

NATALIE GUZMAN

Senior Vice President, Marketing and Public Relations, Fifth Third Bank

I have had many mentors throughout my life. Sometimes, these have been formal and sometimes informal. They have taken on various forms through various relationships and I didn't always know at the time that mentoring was actually occurring.

One of those unconscious mentoring relationships has actually been the most impactful. My mom saw early in her marriage that if she wanted to change the direction of our lives, she needed to obtain a college degree. While working full time and taking care of the home, she would put me and my brother to bed and study from 9 pm to 2 am every night. At a young age, she would tell me why it was important for me to get my education and to go to college. Education became so engrained in my brain that going to college was never a decision, it was just the next step after high school.

As I watched my mom grow in her career and take on various leadership roles, we had many conversations about professionalism, ethics, and business etiquette. I realized in college that my mom was more than my parent, she was also my mentor. I also realized how unique this was as most of my college friends did not have this same type of relationship. My time in college was also when it became apparent that I needed to make sure I was passing along my own experiences to others.

I think that is the real power of mentoring—when we become cognizant of the impact others are having on us and realize that it is not enough to be the recipient, but that we must give back through mentoring others ourselves.

Although I am now in an executive leadership position, mentoring and being mentored is just as important as it was in college and my earlier career. My mom is now retired, however, she is still the person I call when I need professional advice, encouragement or an honest dose of humility, and I am all the better for it

NIKKI LEWALLEN
Executive Director, Rainmakers

Peer mentoring was the start of change for me. And when I say change, it put me on a completely different life path of personal growth and a commitment to greatness. It all started when I joined a local professional organization with a big emphasis on personal development. I remember one of my first meetings being inspired by a man that gave a talk which had a summary like this: "*Always surround yourself with people who are better than you. They will push you. You will learn from them."* Another one of my first meetings, the speakers' message was: *"Make sure you do something every day that scares you. Push yourself outside your comfort zone."* That day, I just so happened to be sitting at a table with a lady who was a coach. She leaned over to me, seeing that I was totally inspired, and said, *"What is one thing you can commit to, today? I will hold you accountable to get it done."* That day, I made a commitment to face my fear of public speaking. I had an opportunity sitting in front of me to speak to a group of nearly 100 people at an upcoming professional group. I took the challenge, scared to death, and pulled it off. That day was my baseline for public speaking and facing fear plus that coach is now a lifetime mentor and friend. Today, public speaking is part of my daily career. It started with inspiration from peers and the magic of a mentor, encouraging me and holding me accountable.

Mentoring people, especially the next generation, is something I find incredibly rewarding. I love to find people with a passion for greatness, whether they know exactly what they want to do or are clueless - the passion fuels our relationship. To help someone find his or her "Why" in life and set goals to achieve those goals is incredibly rewarding. We have developed an internship program that has enabled me to really commit to mentoring at a deeper level with structured accountability. I encourage all of us, women leaders, to create a system in business, like an internship program, to pay it forward. The growth and joy that interns have brought to my life is immeasurable.

LAURA HAYNES

Senior Vice President, Commercial Banking

I was very fortunate to be raised in a typical "nuclear family" that consisted of my parents, me and younger brother. My brother and I were raised to be strong and independent. Chores were handed out equally and standards were to be met.

College proved to be a time of great awakening. I'm from the south. You were taught early on that you didn't question authority. Answering with "Yes, Sir" and "Yes, Ma'am" was a must. However, in college, teachers were not as structured as the ones I had in high school and I was unable to discuss this with them. In addition to this, I was pulled in several different directions trying to coordinate school, jobs, organizational activities, etc. Not knowing what to do, I turned back to my parents.

My father and mother taught me how to take a step back, evaluate situations and put things in perspective. I didn't need to take things at "face value".

Conversation/communication, in a professional manner, is the key. If a teacher was unable to help, it was fine to go to the Dean. I also did not have to be responsible for handling every job/activity by myself. It is okay to ask for assistance and/or delegate authority.

This guidance has served me well as my career has progressed. In order to evaluate situations, I have learned how to listen to people and watch their body language. I had a mentor who was very good at doing this. She was able to address situations very effectively as a result.

I am, admittedly, not a risk-taker. There have been several times within my career…and life…that I have had to decide whether or not to take a different path to advance my career or to support my family. In those instances, my mentors have been indispensable. They have helped me evaluate my options. The ultimate decision is always mine but the perspective they provide is indispensable.

MONA EULER

Vice President of Neuroscience, IU Health

I am a registered nurse who went to nursing school with the desire to take care of patients but also knew I had leadership instincts. After I graduated from nursing school, I worked hard and moved up the ranks very quickly and found myself a CEO of a small hospital at the young age of 31. I must admit I had wanted the position but at the same time needed a female mentor for guidance or at least to be able to listen to my struggles and tell me I was not alone.

Fourteen years ago, I was one of the few healthcare woman CEO's in Indianapolis and that presented some unique challenges in itself. Luckily enough, I had the guts to step up to the plate at meetings wherein I was one of usually two female executives in the room at times. I still remember the look of shock when I would sit down to lunch with a group of men and just join right into their conversation. I think some of them admired my guts and the others would have rather I sat in the back of the room. Looking back, I don't think I would have changed a thing but really wished there was someone to talk with about those situations.

In addition to the stress and pressure of running the hospital, I had two small children and was in school studying for my masters.

I reached out to the only other woman hospital CEO in Indianapolis and basically called her up and asked if she could spend some time with me for mentoring. To my surprise she said *"Yes"* and that proved to be a pivotal moment in my career. Her name was Anne and we started meeting first in her office at dinners. She gave me tips and advice which was crucial in my development as a leader. She had been in my shoes and offered me suggestions that inspired me to move forward in my career path. I felt safe confiding in her and knew she would share her experiences and mistakes which some leaders are afraid to do because they feel it points out weakness.

Besides professional wisdom, I also received her personal insight. When I asked her if she had any regrets in her career she replied, *"Just one, I let my work come before my personal happiness, it delayed my meeting a partner in marriage and prevented me from having a family. Don't let that happen to you."* I remember that quote even to this day and try as hard as I can to find the balance between a fulfilling career and having a great husband and kids.

Over the years, I have tried my best to give back as a mentor because of the lessons I learned without a mentor and the difference it made when I did find the right person. Not only did I join mentoring organizations but I also have guided relatives and co-workers throughout their careers.

Although Anne moved out of my area and has advanced in her career. I owe my mentor a debt of gratitude that I cannot ever repay.

WENDY MILES

Executive Vice President, Miles Printing

I am a 44 year old woman and mentoring was not something I was introduced to or had thought about. This changed three years ago when I was asked to participate in a formal mentoring program at our company to be a mentor to someone else.

I was asked to mentor to my boss's son Bert, whom I have come to dearly care for. A year after that, his father Bob became my mentor. I have learned much about leadership from my time spent with Bob as my formal mentor. I have also learned by observing his incredible leadership. He knows every employee by name. He's made it a point to become familiar with those little details about others that makes them feel special. He's one of the owners of this 26 million dollar company, but somehow he always makes time to rein in a group to sing "Happy Birthday" to a colleague in our office. He is never too busy to make time for anyone here or to lend an ear to whoever needs him. His door is always open.

Just over a year ago, my mentor Bob was diagnosed with ALS or Amyotrophic Lateral Sclerosis; an illness that has no known cure at present time. When he made the announcement about his illness to the company in the summer of 2012, we were all devastated. Bob is just one of those people who can motivate others with a single word, his tone of voice and his positive energy. He's been a formidable leader for all 140 of us in the company over the years. He's the hub of our wheel if you will. I have to say, at the moment of his announcement, it felt as if the wheels had just fallen off the wagon and we could no longer move. As his mentee and friend, when this announcement was made, I felt such heaviness in my heart for him, his family, his son (my mentee) and the company we are both a part of; that I chose to stay home the next day. I could not stop the tears and the grief was a bit overwhelming for me. However, since that time, I've had the privilege to continue to meet with him during our formal mentor/mentee meetings (which he has been happily willing to continue with), share in a warm felt hug periodically or just chat about whatever comes to mind. More importantly, my colleagues and I have been given the gift of being able to still see him most days as he continues to come to the office - cane in hand, head a bit heavy, but a smile on his face. He has shared with me that this company is a blessing he has and will never take light of.

He is handling this disease with brave determination, boldness and a courageous attitude. This is what I call true mentoring. He is living out the example of what he has professed to be important to him. I am watching his words in action…and this is something I will never forget. He has taught me to take more risks, be thankful for what God has given me, be appreciative of every person who works with me within the company, put family first, and to be more authentic with who I am and my convictions. Through his stories about his past mistakes, he has taught me that it is indeed true…pride does come before a fall. He has reiterated time and time again that remaining humble is a key to success in life, work and in relationships. He has mentioned many times that if we truly believe that the leadership position we have is a gift, then we need to take that gift seriously and consider ourselves blessed stewards versus taking credit or being boastful about where we are. Bob is an incredible man and truly has mentored all of his employees in some way, shape or form. He, even now, continues to be an exemplary example of a strong and grounded leader. I will take all that I have learned from him with me. He and his spirit will forever live in my heart.

ANDREA MOORE

Senior Consultant, Flashpoint HR Consulting

Early in my career, I was fortunate to have in my boss, Ken Jochum, a tremendous ally and mentor. Over the course of our working together (Ken always referred to me as his "colleague"), Ken put me in a position to stretch and grow; he harnessed my natural enthusiasm and people-development skills and helped me to hone them by encouraging opportunities to take risks and try new things. As I reflect on our relationship, I would sum it up as this: I said, *"This is what I want to do,"* and Ken said, *"Let's make that happen."*

Just out of graduate school, I was working as an HR generalist for a global electronics distribution company. I had been with the organization for nine months, and during that time I increasingly noticed opportunities for a more progressive and strategic approach to human resources; in particular, I saw a critical need for a centralized approach to employee learning and leadership development, as the organization was in the midst of dramatic change. When I was told that we had hired Ken to serve as the vice president of human resources and that he was interested in "taking our department to the next level," I felt a sense of optimism and looked forward to meeting with him.

Right out of the gate Ken asked a lot of questions. He had a rich, deep background with large, global employers such as Abbott Laboratories and Shell, and yet rather than telling us what we needed to improve, he asked what we thought. I didn't realize the value in this approach at the time, but upon reflection I now see that that this is how he got the best from his people— he empowered me to step up, and as I did, my natural gift and talents emerged. He gave me opportunities very early in my career that many don't get at any point.

During one of our initial meetings, I shared my ideas for a centralized learning function. I described what I had seen in my short tenure with the company. I had a lot of ambition and more enthusiasm than anyone in the department, and yet, my only experience in leading a learning function came through the knowledge I had gained in my graduate studies. However, I was committed and Ken saw that, so as I shared my ideas he basically said "ok" with a big smile on his face. Over the next few years, together and with the team we established, we built a solid model for learning and development.

Ken excelled naturally as a mentor; he recognized the areas in which I needed direction because of my lack of experience, and at the same time he allowed me to step out and take risks along the way. He was a constant ambassador of my development and growth and pushed me to be my best. In 1999, he sponsored my participation in a full-week change management certification in Manchester, England. Two other HR leaders and I were the only ones participating in the process; we were charged with leading the global change management initiative, and my first major opportunity was facilitating a workshop with 20 CEOs from our European businesses. It was my first corporate training experience, and I was facilitating to an important group of stakeholders—but Ken had complete faith that I was up for it. I even remember a conversation about the workshop and how laissez-faire he was about it. He saw the potential in me and because of the opportunities he provided, my natural strengths emerged.

Over the next few years, Ken encouraged my participation in dozens of certifications and learning events. At 28 years old, I was leading a global team of learning professionals, had countless certifications, and had traveled globally facilitating organizational development initiatives. It is because of this experience that I was able to transition to consulting at age 30 and have continued to hone my craft since that time.

JENNY ANCHONDO
Morning News Anchor

Having only lived in a small town in northern Idaho for the first 20 years of my life, I found myself smack dab in the middle of New York City the summer before my senior year in college. I'd been selected as one of 20 International Radio & Television Society Foundation Fellows and took this as my personal invitation to make the world my oyster.

I figured this was my chance. My big break to "make something" of myself, or at least, learn what it took to actually get a job in journalism after graduation. To do that, I would need help in the form of an uneven relationship. I would need someone who I could probably give nothing back to, to give me their time. I was a first generation college student who knew very little about the business world and even less about attaining my dream job.

For as long as I can remember, I'd wanted to become a broadcast journalist. I knew that NYC, the #1 television market in the country, was supposed to hold the best of the best and I made it my goal to meet with each and every News Director in the New York City market while I was there.

Only now do I realize what a lofty, if not pretentious goal that was. News Directors are not only in charge of hiring, but managing everything else in the newsroom. However, with ignorance as my bliss, I set out to pick their brains and find out what they were looking for in a new employee.

By the end of the summer, each of the five local New York affiliate News Directors had met with me and given me mini mentor sessions. I simply offered them the promise that I would listen and learn from what they told me. They gave generously of their time and they didn't have to say it for me to know; they were probably paying it forward because someone else had helped them.

They reviewed my homemade "news stories" and kindly offered advice without judgment. They explained the specific qualities they were looking for; hard-working, natural, conversational, tenacious journalists who bring something unique to the table.

They offered exercises to help me with my squeaky voice and they suggested revisions for my stories, to make them more compelling.

But most importantly, they let me into their world. I left New York City a little less clueless than I was when I arrived. For that, I'm forever grateful.

These people had a profound impact on me. I've now been from Washington to Arizona to Indiana anchoring the news and doing what I love and I have the people who mentored me, knowing I couldn't give anything back, to thank for that.

I consider everyone who has offered me sound career advice to be a mentor. Whether they spent 15 minutes or several hours with me, their time was golden. Now, as often as possible, I try to do the same.

ELCIRA VILLARREAL, PHD
Senior Consultant, Mentoring Women's Network

I retired in 2012 after a twenty-one year long career - first, as a scientist and later in management. Looking back on my career, I realize that by the time I arrived at Eli Lilly and Company in 1990, I had already acquired many of the skills that would make me successful in a corporate setting - thanks to the teachings of my mother, the best mentor I ever had.

My mother was born in 1916 in the Republic of Panama. She was an orphan by the age of seven and had to move to another city with relatives she had never met. Despite the loss of her parents at an early age and the limitation of only a 6th grade education, she has always had a positive attitude and a passion for life. I would say that these have been her greatest gifts to me. In addition to modeling these two attributes, there are a number of other very important life and career lessons I learned from my mother and that contributed to my success in life and in the corporate world.

I remember vividly, as a child I would come crying to my mom when someone had hurt my feelings and she would comfort me and would always end the discussion with the phrase, *"Just remember, you are not better than anyone, but no one is better than you."* At those times, I did not understand why she would always say that, but later on, I came to realize that she was laying the foundation for the concept of respect for others and self-respect. *"You must always treat others with respect, but must also ensure that others treat you with respect."*

At a time when women in Panama usually stayed home, my mother worked at the Colon Free Zone, the largest state organization in Colon. She started as an administrative assistant and rose through the ranks to become Director of the Human Resources Department. Early on, I got the message that women could have careers and be leaders. She was also very good at setting her priorities and even though she took her job very seriously, my sister and I were her highest priorities in life. She had a clear understanding of work/life balance even then.

Another concept that my mother modeled was that everything is about relationships. She would try her best to get along with everyone but would deal swiftly and effectively with conflict if it arose. She would always approach situations with a win-win attitude. She always allowed others to save face. She would always say, *"No one likes to lose face. Even if you are right, you should always allow the other person to save face. If you press your point and the other person loses face, you may have won in that moment, but you will have an enemy for life."*

Through her example, she taught me that you must always care for your employees and get to know them as well as allowing them to know you. She adhered to the principle that you cannot lead or follow those that you do not know. If you are able to show the people you lead that you genuinely care about them, they will give you their best and even listen to the harshest feedback.

My mother understood the value of networking very clearly and would always tie it to the concepts of reciprocity and gratitude. Her philosophy was that you should always be of help if you could without expecting something in return. She did not work in a silo but had deep connections throughout the organization. She believes that life is reciprocal and that the good that you do always comes back to you in one way or another. She always operates from a mindset of abundance versus scarcity.

Leading by example was one of my mother's trademarks. I never saw her ask one of her employees to do something that she would not be willing to do herself. When she was wrong about something or if a project did not go well, she would be the first one to admit it and instead of punishing herself for the mistake, she would spend her energy figuring out how to fix it and how to do it differently the next time. My mother would always share her good and bad experiences at work during dinner.

One of the biggest gifts she modeled was that you should always feel comfortable no matter the circumstances. She would say that you should be equally comfortable in the home of the poorest person in Panama as well as in the home of the richest person. This lesson has been very useful to me throughout my life when I had to meet with high level executives to discuss my projects, serving on community boards, and as I engage in new endeavors.

My mother is now 97 years old and I will be forever grateful to her for the valuable lessons that allowed me as a woman, as a Latina, and as a lesbian to successfully navigate the corporate world.

TAMARA ZAHN

2013-2014 Chairperson, International Downtown Association

Ancora Imparo. I feel like Michelangelo, who at the age of 87 in 1562, said "Ancora imparo, (I am still learning)."

I recently started the fourth chapter of my life. I completed the first three chapters – growing up: advancing my career; and reaching some level of achievement – with a great deal of hard work, growth, and inventing as I went.

I have tried to give generously of my time and talent. I have been a mentor and I have offered wisdom and also provided connections whenever possible. So, it wasn't until I recently spoke at the Mentoring Women's Network that I was temporarily speechless. Who were my mentors? I was asked for one of the first times that I can remember.

Who were my mentors? That's a good question. Who are the people that has inspired me, taught me, challenged me and supported me? Who are the people that has given me that extra time or boost that helped define who I am today?

As I reflect on my life and my career, I am grateful for a large number of people who have helped me along the way. I am certainly thankful for having a cast of caring champions – teachers, parents, and a husband (that I will nominate for best husband in the world anytime). I am also sure that I couldn't have achieved what I did without many, many business mentors along the way. I am especially appreciative of board chairs, Mayors, Deputy Mayors, peers and others who taught me, guided me, and supported me during the last twenty years in ways that I am forever indebted.

I am particularly appreciative of the unwavering support and honest feedback of my friend, Taylor Estes. I've known Taylor for nearly thirty years. We were both living in New Orleans back then, although, we didn't meet there. We both happened to fall in love with Hoosier men, and that's how our paths came together.

Taylor has been there for me at every major decision and milestone. She encouraged me to give up the east coast life I enjoyed and to move to Indianapolis. She (and her mom) advocated for me, at the age of 39, to marry the man I had dated on and off for years. Less than a year later, she spent hours talking with me about the opportunity to take an enormous risk and start up a new not-for-profit, Indianapolis Downtown, Inc. I must say her advice has been extraordinary.

Taylor has counseled, comforted and humored me through good times and bad. She has inspired me to reach and achieve. She has coached me to shake it off and know when to speak up or bite my tongue. We have laughed together and cried together. She knows me well and she isn't afraid to point out when I'm getting in my own way.

Now that I've been asked the question and I'm inventing the fourth chapter of my life, I'm learning! Ancora Impara! And I am seeking more mentors who can impart their wisdom and their secrets to their success and well-being. You can be sure that I will continue to enjoy and cherish Taylor and the many that have mentored me along the way.

MARIETTA STALCUP

President, Lead Denovo

I, like many women I know, have had an interesting relationship with this concept called mentoring. As a high-potential individual at a top 10 pharmaceutical company I was assigned a mentor. While this effort was very much appreciated and well-intentioned, it was less than effective for several reasons - but the most important was I never felt a connection to those assigned to me. At the time, I am not sure I truly understood how to be a great mentee and this is critical for a successful mentoring partnership.

This all changed when I read several articles about the concept of a "Personal Board of Directors." It seemed to hit home with me that I did not need one mentor assigned to me by my company, I needed several mentors – inside and outside the company – with whom I connected with at a level that allowed me to hear their words of wisdom. I learned how to be a great mentee and how to build long-term relationships. I am very fortunate as today, I have about eight outstanding mentors. Some I speak with monthly, and others just as needed but they each serve a unique role and bring value in their own area of expertise. More importantly, they want to help me – they truly want me to succeed. They have my best interests at heart and they are doing it not because someone has asked, but because they truly want to help.

Knowledge leads to self-empowerment. My mentors provide me with the right knowledge at the right time and in doing so empower me to achieve my potential.

SARAH BETH AUBREY
Principal, Prosperity Consulting, LLC

I was 23 and green. Literally, I was green around the gills from riding in Chicago's stop and go rush-hour traffic. My new boss was maneuvering his Suburban like a bulldozer and I felt a nasty case of carsickness sweeping over me as I tried to read aloud the directions I'd prepared. We were running late and I sensed he thought it was my fault. Problem was, David, one of the impressive and intimidating co-founders of the consulting firm I'd just been hired into, was not listening. I'd tell him one thing and he's promptly dismiss it saying: *"It couldn't possibly be right".* I should have felt bad about the supposedly shoddy directions, but I thought *he* was wrong and my own 'type-A' personality was perilously close to surfacing!

Suddenly noticing my nausea, David put both front windows down. *"Are you gonna puke?"* he queried. I guess he didn't look sympathetic enough or maybe the last thing I wanted to admit was how close I was to tossing my coffee all over my new suit. Either way, I lost my composure….Without thinking about it, I impulsively wadded the directions and threw them across David's view and out his window. *"I'd feel fine if I thought you were listening!"* I exclaimed. *"Uh-Oh."* was all I could think.

After nearly rear-ending the compact in front of us, David recovered and glowered over at me. I pressed on. *"We didn't need those anyway and you need to turn around,"* I said, albeit meekly. David's scowl burst into a massive grin then he bellowed with laughter. As he moved to change lanes, he kept laughing. *"Yes Ma'am!"*

We finally arrived at the client's location. There were four men to whom David promptly relayed the direction-tossing story. I was appalled. The group laughed. Later that week at the sales meeting, David relayed the story to the whole team, again all are men and all are much more experienced than I. He capped off the tale with a public apology to me. *"Don't ever let me find any one of you guy's treating her like I did. Sarah, I apologize. Here's a professional that wants her voice to be heard. You know what-she was right about the directions, too!"*

I went on to work with David for three more years and he probably relayed the story 50 more times. He had a knack for using it just when he sensed people were about to underestimate me for my age or gender. Today, he lives on the West Coast and I see him a couple times a year. He's written recommendations, made phone calls on my behalf, attended awards banquets, and served on my company advisory board. It's been over 10 years since I worked for him, but he has always encouraged me to do one thing: make my voice heard.

ELIZABETH CISCO

System Executive, Marketing, St. Vincent Health

As I reflect upon how I have been mentored throughout both my professional and personal life, I gravitate to those individuals with whom I developed a trusting, enlightening, educational and mutual relationship. These individuals and the bonds we built together span the past 30 plus years and includes a diverse grouping including my high school yearbook teacher, to a personal trainer with whom I worked out for 10 years, to a dear friend who shared an interest in biking and antiques, to a wise and intellectually curious man who is one of my direct reports, to my wonderful husband and many others. And at times, I am surprised from whom I may learn some of the most important aspects of life - such as from my son and eldest stepson.

One individual stands out for me, and this individual helped me grow in ways in which I wasn't even aware that I was capable. This person took the time to understand me … to learn who I really was based on my work and personal experiences, my family dynamics, my dreams and aspirations, as well as my weaknesses and opportunities for growth and maturity. This person taught me to push myself, to get smarter, to look at situations from a different angle and to know there were myriad possibilities for me to explore and to become a more well-rounded professional woman.

Most importantly, this individual allowed me the opportunity to be who I was and to grow into who I have become professionally based on a refreshingly open approach that allows me to be me without fear of not being exactly who or what I was 'supposed' to be – to celebrate the woman that I was and am. Even during times of difficulty, I continue to feel the basis of what this person taught me and to be strong within so that I am able to fully serve others with whom I work and play.

Because of how I have been mentored and been supported by this individual and many others, I feel a strong desire and responsibility to mentor individuals who want to learn as well as to expand upon their areas of focus and passion. Mentoring, to me, is about relationships and fostering those relationships to ensure you help guide others to understand their strengths, talents, uniqueness and ability to grow in directions that are intentional, exciting, challenging and fulfilling. And more often than not, you are rewarded by learning as much from them as they do from you.

Diane Maydee Mandal

Senior Exam Coach, Founder of StuffedNurse, Lifelong Learner

I have always considered myself to be a very curious soul with an insatiable appetite for challenges and something new - but what and who I am now is a product of all the encounters and interactions with different people I have had the privilege to cross paths with. I will mention 3 mentors that I've had (and still have as my mentors within me to this day), they are my 3rd grade teacher, a fisherman I met randomly, and a person I currently work with.

My 3rd grade teacher believed in me and taught me the value of believing in myself, plus lots more. I had low self-esteem and was a mediocre student before I met her but with her trust in me, in just a few short months, I was performing at the top of the class and even was the school's representative at various competitions.

One time, at a math competition, I caught her tutoring one of the contestants from a rival school. I felt so betrayed because she was my coach and class adviser so I proceeded to have a mini tantrum (hey, I was only 10 at that time). She told me something that still rings in my ears up to this day, "*When you share what you know to others, you'll get so much more in return*" and also, "*No one can take what is within you, teaching someone else is giving yourself a chance to be your best self.*" Of course during that time, I did not get what those words mean.

I also noticed that she is doing something else to me. Given the fact that I have a bit of a reclusive personality, she might have thought/planned that it would be great to enroll me in a peer tutoring program, where kids teach other kids on a subject that they excel at. I did not know at that time that she was healing my self-esteem issues as well as teaching me the value of sharing what you know so you can help yourself be a better person while also training others. I learned how to speak publicly and overcome my stutter. I learned the joy of seeing someone excel in something I helped them at, and that gave me immense confidence and a sense of can-do-attitude which I share to my students up to this day.

Maybe it was her that inspired me to be an educator and a coach, or maybe she saw the potential in me and cultivated it. I shall be grateful to her forever for laying down the foundation of my teaching and mentoring career.

Another person who had a deep impact on how and who I am now is a fisherman I met on one of my provincial forays years ago. He only had 2nd grade education but he can hold his candle amongst the PhDs I usually mingle with in terms of philosophy and human wisdom. I asked him how come he knows so much and has so much knowledge considering that he had no access to higher education(?). He said, "*I listen*"- those two words hold so much weight. Through him, I learned the value of listening even to those who may seem to know less than me, and I reap the benefits of that on a frequent basis now. Yes, I do have an 'uneducated' fisherman as one of my go-to person when I need some soul-food. What he taught me about listening is one of the keys as to why I am effective in what I do now coaching people.

The third person is someone that I work with. She is one of the persons I really admire and hold as one of my life teachers even though she may not know it. Working in the field of academics and exam preparation, we handle achievers and ultra-driven individuals who of course are often with a strong personality as well. She always handles them and all their issues with grace. There are times that she could have easily fired someone or issued a memo since she held the position to do so but she never did. Working with her made me initially think that she is a weakling, but of course that is not the case. The way she handles conflict and people taught me that leading is more in the actions, which is her primary strength. Her approach transformed me from a critic to a fan by teaching me (through modeling) how to handle myself and people with a gentle grace and manner. She was and still is unfailingly gentle to me even if my rebellious streak makes me go against her at times (she's my boss). I can really say that the time I spent with her so far made me a better individual inside and out. She is one of the 'soft' female leaders with a core of steel who I know and highly admire.

I'm not sure if I can claim that I really mentored someone in my mere 28 years of existence in this world, but I do often get messages of thanks from previous students (who are often much older than me) and acquaintances that they are using the things I taught them from 1, 3, 5, up to 6 years ago (Huh? I can't even remember what I taught them, ahaha). I guess that is what mentoring is all about, making an impact on someone's life for the better.

Mentoring knows no boundaries, transcends cultural borders, and does not care about class in society nor age. It is all about learning from one another, no matter what age or gender.

We are all students of the University of Life. Those three individuals may not know that they have mentored me and yet they all served as catalysts for making me a better individual at different stages in my life.

If unconscious mentoring can have such a great impact, as their actions had on me, and as my random snippets of helping out had on my students and acquaintances, just think of how much more can active mentoring do to empower someone, or change the world.

Mentoring is a gift that keeps on giving, just sharing your life and having the intent to help someone can have a tremendous impact on how they would turn out to be. Perhaps mentoring is the gateway to a whole new better world for everyone in the near future - a legacy that I want to help bring forth and leave as a testament of having a life of learning and teaching.

ABOUT THE AUTHOR

Alison Martin-Books is the Founder, President and CEO of
Mentoring Women's Network, an organization whose mission is
a community of empowered women developing one another
personally and professionally through mentoring relationships.

With impressive background work and roughly 14 years in nonprofit (beginning with four years working in higher education
and on to Executive Director at two different health-related
nonprofit organizations) Alison Martin-Books has excelled in all
areas of leadership and communication. While performing under
the great pressure with roles advancing from Youth Market Director to Corporate Events Director, to Executive Director, and
to Development Vice President, Martin-Books inhabited poise
and confidence, leading to organizational success. A gifted fundraiser, Alison managed continued growth of a 2.4 million dollar
local campaign and secured national gifts totaling 3.5 million
dollars.

Her commitment to her passion for education, developing female leaders and to giving back to the community lead her to
launch Mentoring Women's Network and the virtual mentoring
program development. She acts as a liaison to a national com-

mittee responsible for the marketing and content for the national platform and consults with corporations on the development and strategy aligned with leadership development programs and initiatives for emerging female leaders and works to develop meaningful partnerships with companies wishing to develop and promote female talent.

She is married with two children and a stepson and serves on the board for Integrating Woman Leaders and volunteers for The Little Red Door and The American Heart Association's Go Red for Women Luncheon.

To learn more about Mentoring Women's Network and The Mentoring Women's Network Foundation, visit www.mentoringwomensnetwork.com